Journey into God

Journey into God

Spiritual Reflections for Travelers

Mark G. Boyer

WIPF & STOCK · Eugene, Oregon

JOURNEY INTO GOD
Spiritual Reflections for Travelers

Copyright © 2022 Mark G. Boyer. All rights reserved. Except for brief quotations in critical publications or reviews, no part of this book may be reproduced in any manner without prior written permission from the publisher. Write: Permissions, Wipf and Stock Publishers, 199 W. 8th Ave., Suite 3, Eugene, OR 97401.

Wipf & Stock
An Imprint of Wipf and Stock Publishers
199 W. 8th Ave., Suite 3
Eugene, OR 97401

www.wipfandstock.com

PAPERBACK ISBN: 978-1-6667-3364-8
HARDCOVER ISBN: 978-1-6667-2847-7
EBOOK ISBN: 978-1-6667-2848-4

JANUARY 7, 2022 10:29 AM

The Scripture quotations contained herein are from the New Revised Standard Version Bible, copyright © 1989 by the Division of Christian Education of the National Council of the Churches of Christ in the U.S.A., and are used by permission. All rights reserved.

Dedicated to
Irene Natalie Villmer,
a fellow Old Miner,
and a companion on the journey.

Sustain your family always in your kindness,
O Lord, we pray,
correct them, set them in order,
graciously protect them under your rule,
and in your unfailing goodness
direct them along the way of salvation.
Through Christ our Lord. Amen.
—*THE ROMAN MISSAL*, 1124

Contents

Abbreviations | viii

Introduction | xi

1 Journey | 1

2 Road | 19

3 Path | 43

4 Route, Highway, Gateway | 56

5 Walk | 70

6 Way | 102

7 Conclusion: Journey Themes in *The Roman Missal* | 116

Bibliography | 151

Recent Books by Mark G. Boyer published by Wipf & Stock | 155

Abbreviations

BCE = Before the Common Era (same as BC = Before Christ)

CB (NT) = Christian Bible (New Testament)

Acts = Acts of the Apostles
Col = Letter to the Colossians
2 Cor = Second Letter of Paul to the Corinthians
Heb = Letter to the Hebrews
John = John's Gospel
Luke = Luke's Gospel
Mark = Mark's Gospel
Matt = Matthew's Gospel
2 Pet = Second Letter of Peter
Rev = Revelation
2 Tim = Second Letter to Timothy

CE = Common Era (same as AD = *Anno Domini*, in the year of the Lord)
cf. = confer, compare

HB (OT) = Hebrew Bible (Old Testament)

Amos = Amos
Dan = Daniel
Deut = Deuteronomy

Abbreviations

Eccl – Ecclesiastes
Exod = Exodus
Ezek = Ezekiel
Gen = Genesis
Hab = Habakkuk
Hos = Hosea
Isa = Isaiah
Jer = Jeremiah
Job = Job
Jonah = Jonah
Josh = Joshua
Judg = Judges
1 Kgs = First Book of Kings
2 Kgs = Second Book of Kings
Lam = Lamentations
Lev = Leviticus
Mal = Malachi
Mic = Micah
Neh = Nehemiah
Num = Numbers
Prov = Proverbs
Ps(s) = Psalm(s)
Ruth = Ruth
1 Sam = First Book of Samuel
2 Sam = Second Book of Samuel
Zech = Zechariah
Zeph = Zephaniah

OT (A) = Old Testament (Apocrypha)

Bar = Baruch
1 Esd = First Book of Esdras
2 Esd = Second Book of Esdras
Jdt = Judith

Abbreviations

1 Macc = Frist Book of Maccabees
2 Macc = Second Book of Maccabees
Sg Three = Prayer of Azariah (Song of Three Jews)
Sir = Sirach (Ecclesiasticus)
Sus = Susanna
Tob = Tobit
Wis = Wisdom (of Solomon)

par(s) = paragraph(s)
RM = *The Roman Missal*

Introduction

Spirituality of Journey Steps

THIS IS A BOOK about spirituality, more specifically, the spiritual journey. Before beginning any journey or trip—spiritual or otherwise—we experience a state of order. We have a job, a home in which we live, safety, security, identity, relationships, and all else that we name to be good. Then comes the call to journey, to travel, to take a trip, to walk, to pilgrimage, to hit the road, etc. The call to begin a journey may come from an urge within us; it may be an invitation from a spouse or a friend to fly somewhere; it may be as simple as taking the dog for a walk in the neighborhood, even taking different streets! The call disrupts our ordered lives. We enter into chaos as soon as we prepare for our excursion. We have to pack a suitcase; we have to get a neighbor to watch our home; we have to get someone to

Introduction

take the dog; we have to stop the mail; we have to pay all bills which will become due while we are gone; we have to leave the house; etc. According to McColman, "first [we] recognize the call; then [we] prepare for the journey, then [we] embark on the adventure."[1] In other words, by entering into the stage of chaos, we enter into the process of transformation.

We enter liminal space, that is, living in between the order we had before we prepared and left and the new disorder we will experience on the way and the new disorder we will live once we have arrived at our destination. Paintner, referencing John Cassian, says that three renunciations are required for the spiritual journey. The first renunciation "is our former way of life . . . . The second is the inner practice of asceticism and letting go of our mindless thoughts. The third renunciation is to let go of our image of God and to recognize that any image or pronouncement we can ever make about God is much too small to contain the divine."[2] In the liminal phase of our journey, we encounter conflict, inconsistencies, darkness. We get to the airport to discover that our flight was cancelled, and we need to stand in line to rebook for another flight. We get on the road and a tire on our car goes flat. We walk out the front door with the dog, and we discover that our street is being repaved; we have to take a different route. Or, the sidewalk is blocked, and we have to turn around or take a side street into unknown territory. We may turn around and retreat in order to begin again later, because the chaotic disorder is too threatening.

After having conquered step-by-step the preliminary stage of the journey—getting out of the house and to our destination—we experience more disorderly chaos. Our plane may arrive too late to be met by a representative from our tour company. We have to wait in line to have our passports checked before we can enter the foreign country and miss our train, taxi, or bus. The hotel may not be what we expected. We may find ourselves in a different hotel in a different city every two days with a different map of where things are located. We cannot find the same over-the-counter medicine for headaches or constipation that we take at home. We are at the mercy of the hotel for breakfast and dinner; we are at the mercy of the travel agent leading our group concerning when we need to get out of bed, when we need to be on the motor coach, where we stop for breaks, and what we see at the next destination. Finally, we finish the journey and head

---

1. McColman, *Answering*, 13.
2. Paintner, *Soul*, 114.

Introduction

home, only to encounter more of the chaotic disorder—in airports, traffic, and coaches—that we did in getting to our destination.

When we arrive home and walk through the door into our house, we realize that we have been changed. We have experienced reordering. We have been transformed mentally, emotionally, psychologically, physically, sexually, aesthetically, and spiritually. Some aspects of our life may be more transformed than others. Our reordered status means that we will never be the same again because we took a journey, a trip, a pilgrimage, a walk, etc. Rohr calls this a crossover moment, "after which a person will never be the same again. Somewhere, somehow the challenge comes that sets us on a different path: the path of purpose, the path of integrity, the path of transcendence that lifts us—heart, mind, and soul—above the pitiable level of the comfortable and the mundane."[3] As we settle into our new ordered life, a new feeling of life-is-good envelopes us. It is OK to be who we have become because of our journey. We may have a greater knowledge of our identity; we may have new friends made on the coach or in the hotel; we may have a new perspective on the new countries we visited; we may feel more secure as we continue to live our new lives.

Whether or not we realize it, from a spiritual perspective, we can attribute the transformation to God, the divine presence. We may not have considered our road trip to have anything to do with the divine or the spiritual, but just because we did not recognize God's presence doesn't mean that the divine was not there! Because we exist in the very One—no matter what name we give—to whom we journey, every travel, pilgrimage, or walk is done in the divine presence. Every step we take on the sidewalk, every flight to another country, every tour we are a part of, every cross-country road trip is a call to leave order, enter disorder, reorder, and be transformed in the process. We engage in this over and over and over again throughout our lives.

The journeys are preparation for the final call to leave order, enter liminal chaos and go, and, hopefully, to finish on the other side of death, basking in the divine presence as a transformed self. There is no need to distinguish a journey from a pilgrimage, as is often done by overtly religious people! It makes no difference if we walk, race, explore, pilgrimage, journey, path-find, trail-blaze, or road trip. Even the famous travel magnate, Rick Steves, states, "If I was to measure profit, it is on how transformational

---

3. Rohr, "Politics."

Introduction

the travel is."[4] It makes no difference if we awaken to the divine presence in whom we live and move and have our being. Transformation occurs because we cooperate with God, whether we are aware of it or not. Through a life-time journey, God transforms us in preparation for our final transformation into the divine. And we are not alone in this ongoing process. "Transformed people transform people," states Vaillancourt Murphy.[5] We "can lead people on the spiritual journey [only] as far as [we] have gone," states Rohr.[6] He explains:

> We don't have the ability to lead anybody anywhere new unless we have walked it ourselves to some degree. In general, we can only lead people on the spiritual journey as far as we ourselves have gone.... That's why the best thing we can do for people is to stay on the journey ourselves. We transform people to the degree we have been transformed.[7]

This is the spirituality of journey. The steps consist of (1) order, (2) hearing the call to journey, (3) answering the call to journey by preparation, (4) entering the disordered chaos of taking the journey and being transformed, and (5) coming home reordered and transformed.

Title: *Journey into God: Spiritual Reflections for Travelers*

4. Bruner, "Travel Guru," 21.
5. Hendler-Voss, "Restore Justice," 37.
6. Rohr, "Wounded Healers."
7. Rohr, "God."

Introduction

Journey

The title of this book illustrates and enhances the spirituality of journey: *Journey into God: Spiritual Reflections for Travelers*. The first word in the title of this book is journey. A journey is a "trip somewhere, a trip or expedition from one place to another."[8] It can also be a "process of development, a gradual passing from one state to another regarded as more advanced, e.g., from innocent to mature awareness,"[9] such as a spiritual journey. Shapiro emphasizes that "spirituality is progressive" and, thus, he speaks "of a maturing rather than a mature spirituality." He states that the outer journey "is in fact an inner one." The individual person journeys to the self where he or she knows all is God.[10] McColman reminds us that it was the eighteenth-century writer Oliver Goldsmith who said, "Life is a journey."[11] Sheldrake says, "Spirituality is . . . a journey . . . . [S]pirituality involves a process of transformation that seeks to enable us to move from less adequate values and ways of life to what is more adequate and, indeed, fulfilling in an ultimate sense."[12] According to Poffenberger, "[D]isruption is the starting place for the authentic spiritual journey."[13] Williamson states, "The goal of the spiritual journey is to become a vessel through which God can dream his dream of a more loving world."[14] She adds, "God works through each of us to the extent to which we make ourselves receptive."[15] All human experience is spiritual, no matter how one limits it with descriptive adjectives, like civil, awesome, secular, religious, etc. Because any kind of journey changes us, it is a transformational journey for which, according to Hollis, "we are accountable. We will have numerous things happen to us that push us in one direction or another, and we can spend a lot of our life blaming if we wish to. But in the end, we're responsible for the patterns that unfold and the choices made."[16]

---

8. *Encarta*, 972.
9. *Encarta*, 972.
10. Shapiro, "Roadside Assistance: Holy Land", 47.
11. McColman, *Answering*, xi–xii.
12. Sheldrake, *Spiritual Way*, xi.
13. Poffenberger, "Letter."
14. Kiesling, "New American," 66.
15. Kiesling, "New American," 67.
16. Kiesling, "Personal Accountability," 52.

Introduction

"The goal of the spiritual journey," according to Rohr, "is to discover and move toward connectedness on ever new levels. We may begin by making little connections with other people, with nature and animals, then grow into deeper connectedness with people. Finally, we can experience full connectedness as union with God."[17] Flanagan applies the metaphor of the journey to which the individual is sent "to walk the next stage"[18] to the collective journey of the church. He writes: "Rather than traveling in a straight line, the church in every time and place wanders its way toward the fullness of the reign of God, sometimes receiving God's grace such that the heavens drop down and God's presence is known and felt, and sometimes stumbling as it journeys forth."[19]

Similarly, Senior compares recovery from an illness to "going on a long journey from one world to the next." He continues:

> The impact of illness is equivalent to "leaving home"—saying farewell to what has been familiar to us—and then heading toward a new and as-yet-unknown place that we hope is a "place" of recovery and healing.... In the midst of this process or "journey" one is on the "threshold" between two "worlds." A typical experience during such a "liminal" state, we are told, is isolation, a feeling of being alone.[20]

Even though we may feel alone, we are not. We are in God. According to Shapiro, spirituality is "a progressive stripping away of the conditioning that blinds [us] to the truest fact of [our] existence: [we] are a happening of God, YHVH, ... the Happening happening as all happening."[21] Echoing Rohr, Shapiro states, "Spirituality isn't fixed but fluid, not a final 'aha' but a recurring 'wow.'"[22] In other words, spirituality is a lifetime spiritual pilgrimage.

---

17. Rohr, "Community."
18. Flanagan, *Stumbling*, 179.
19. Flanagan, *Stumbling*, 176.
20. Senior, "This Issue," 218–19.
21. Shapiro, "Roadside Assistance: Holy Land," 47.
22. Shapiro, "Roadside Assistance: Holy Land," 47.

Introduction

Jesus Model

In the Christian Bible (New Testament) Jesus is presented as a model for making a journey in two ways. First, three of the gospels (Mark, Matthew, Luke) present him on a one-year journey around Galilee and Jerusalem. The other gospel, John, gives him a three-year journey of preaching, teaching, and traveling. Thus, the literary motif of journey is clearly present in the life of Jesus. Second, from a doctrinal point of view, Christianity presents him journeying from God to the womb of his mother, Mary. According to the creeds, the only-begotten Son of God came down from heaven and was incarnate of Mary by the Holy Spirit, or conceived by the Holy Spirit and born of Mary.[23] According to the hymn quoted by Paul in his Letter to the Philippians, Jesus, being "in the form of God, emptied himself, . . . being born in human likeness," and "he humbled himself and became obedient to the point of death . . . on a cross." But "God also highly exalted him" (Phil 2:6–9). The hymn illustrates Jesus' journey from God in the world above to the world below and back to the world above. Through his journey to, on, and from earth, Jesus was transformed by his human experience. " . . . [S]piritually transformed people [share] . . . one common denominator," according to Rohr: "[T]hey have all died before they died. They have followed in the self-emptying steps of Jesus, a path from death to life . . . ."[24] Thus, Jesus serves as a model for those on the journey into God.

Into God

The journey is about making our way into God. While "we live and move and have our being" in God (Acts 17:28), we are also traveling throughout our lives into God. Poust states: "A true pilgrimage . . . [is] . . . an interior journey . . . . Life itself is a pilgrimage . . . to the core of [one's] being, to that destination in [one's] heart where God resides."[25] According to McColman, "[T]he Christian journey [is] into the love of God."[26] Shapiro states, " . . . Jesus was a Jewish mystic who came to know what all mystics know, namely,

---

23. RM, 527–28.
24. Rohr, "Five Consoling Messages."
25. Poust, *Everyday Divine*, 149.
26. McColman, *Answering*, xiv.

that all things are a part of God and nothing is apart from God."²⁷ Casey writes, " . . . [O]ur world is in constant communication with the spiritual world and with God, who stands at its center."²⁸ This leads Hubl to state, " . . . [N]othing is not spiritual."²⁹ Likewise, Rohr states: "I know myself and all others to be a part of God . . . . And with this sense of wholeness comes a sense of holiness, a sense of love from and for all beings."³⁰ Williamson explains, "Mature spirituality extends beyond the confines of the narrow self . . . . It's a global and universal phenomenon . . . . But you can't ever evolve beyond a connection to God himself."³¹ The end of the pilgrimage of life is the beginning of new life that exists on the other side of death. "Indeed for your faithful, Lord," we pray in Preface I for the Dead, "life is changed not ended, and, when this earthly dwelling turns to dust, an eternal dwelling is made ready for them in heaven."³² According to Sheldrake, "Christian spiritual traditions all embody a sense of transcendence . . . and point toward a final eternal endpoint for human existence."³³

Spiritual

This book presents *spiritual* reflections for travelers. As an adjective, the word, *spiritual*, basically, refers to aspects of one's spirit. As a noun, the word *spirituality* refers to the quality or condition of being spiritual, that is, being in touch with one's spirit and nurturing it. Shapiro defines spirituality as "the art of exploring [our] nature . . . . [I]t is a direct apprehension of reality outside of words and scripture; a direct pointing to reality and seeing into one's true nature."³⁴ Hollis refers to this as "the encounter with the reality and magnitude of our own souls." He adds, "That kind of dialogue [as a result of the encounter] is not about withdrawing from the world."³⁵ According to Hollis, "the numinous"—God—"is something that solicits [our]

27. Shapiro, "Roadside Assistance: Holy Land," 48.
28. Casey, *Balaam's Donkey*, 325.
29. Hubl, "Lean."
30. Rohr, "A Big Experiment."
31. Kiesling, "New American," 64.
32. RM, 622.
33. Sheldrake, *Spiritual Way*, xi.
34. Shapiro, "Roadside Assistance: Spiritual Traveler," 14.
35. Kiesling, "Personal Accountability," 48.

INTRODUCTION

response." It is "found wherever we are moved and touched—somehow activated psychically."[36] Sheldrake states, "spirituality . . . is a process, a movement, and a journey. . . . [I]t underlines that all Christian spiritual wisdom traditions place an emphasis on growth, development, and transformation . . . . [T]o engage with spirituality is to commit oneself to an intentional and often challenging practice of life."[37]

While the movement of spirit is different for different people, "spiritual things need physical counterparts to convey their message."[38] In other words, spirituality is the "lived experience of contemporary mystics,"[39] us! And because "we are always beginning the spiritual life," always moving from order to chaos to order, "[b]eginning again is about letting ourselves be surprised by God and encountering the familiar with holy wonder."[40] McColman says, "We search for the divine, only to be found by God."[41] He adds, "[T]he God we seek is already present with us, right here and right now . . . . We do not need to go anywhere to get closer to God, for God is closer to us than we are to ourselves."[42] McColman also says, "This [longing for God and God's longing for us—the call to love and participate in love] is a journey without a goal—a journey through a pathless land—but still we walk the path of love."[43] In order to stay on the trail of the pathless journey, we need spiritual practices. Sheldrake explains: "Spiritual practices . . . are regular, disciplined activities that both express a particular vision of life and seek to consolidate this through a framework of meditative action."[44] Rohr states, "Disciplined practice is essential to the spiritual life; yet spiritual attainment is not the result of one's own efforts, but the result of the experience of oneness with Ultimate Reality."[45] Rohr cautions, "We are conditioned to treat the spiritual life as another commodity, rather than

---

36. Kiesling, "Personal Accountability," 51.
37. Sheldrake, *Spiritual Way*, 141.
38. Rohr, "Liminal Time," 5.
39. Rohr, "Big Experiment."
40. Paintner, *Soul*, 98, 106.
41. McColman, *Answering*, 19.
42. McColman, *Answering*, 43–4.
43. McColman, *Answering*, 47.
44. Sheldrake, *Spiritual Way*, 149.
45. Rohr, "Big Experiment."

Introduction

as a discipline of inner transformation with a corresponding commitment to alleviating suffering in the world."[46]

One such disciplined activity or practice is prayer. While many people use the words *prayer* and *meditation* interchangeably, Boylan writes, " . . . [M]editation is only 'thinking about God,' while prayer is 'talking to God.'"[47] He states, " . . . [P]rayer seems . . . to be the result of a progressive intimacy and friendship with God."[48] McColman states, "The contemplative call is a call to intimacy with God."[49] However, McColman considers the use of the word *contemplation* to "refer to silent prayer, centering prayer, meditative prayer, and the prayer of the heart, etc."[50] For McColman, "the heart of the contemplative call [is] the possibility to behold, as an ever-present invitation from the divine mystery. But such beholding is not a task for us to complete; it is a natural state for us to remember."[51] For McColman, beholding "involves gazing, loving, receiving love, a sense of mutuality. We behold God in response to God beholding us. In our beholding, we are transformed."[52] Boylan summarizes this when he writes, " . . . [P]rayer is a supernatural act, and is, therefore, completely dependent on the grace of God."[53]

Another disciplined activity or practice is creativity. Rohr states "that each of [us] has the capacity to offer something new to the world."[54] He writes, "A miraculous event unfolds when we throw the lead of our personal story into the transformative flames of creativity."[55] The steps of this spiritual practice, "this creative alchemy," begin by "first get[ting] still enough to hear what wants to be expressed through us, and then . . . step[ping] out of the way and let[ting] it . . . . Such a space is sacred."[56] In the sacred space of creativity, the "divine core of personality which cannot be separated from God" is revealed. Our supreme purpose in life," writes Rohr, "is . . . to

---

46. Rohr, "Engaged Love."
47. Boylan, *Difficulties*, 17.
48. Boylan, *Difficulties*, xxxvii.
49. McColman, *Answering*, 27.
50. McColman, *Answering*, xiv.
51. McColman, *Answering*, 39.
52. McColman, *Answering*, 97, 99.
53. Boylan, *Difficulties*, 39.
54. Rohr, "Fallow Time."
55. Rohr, "Fallow Time."
56. Rohr, "Fallow Time."

Introduction

discover this spark of the divine that is in our hearts . . . . [T]he divinity within ourselves is one and the same in all." Recognizing the "unbroken awareness of the presence of God in all creatures" leads us to creativity.[57] Thus,

> [w]hen we allow ourselves to be a conduit for creative energy, we experience direct apprehension of that energy. We become a channel for grace. To make art is to make love with the sacred . . . . Artistic self-expression necessitates periods of quietude in which it appears that nothing is happening . . . . We have to incubate inspiration. Art begins with receptivity.[58]

According to Rohr: ". . . [W]e can't manage, maneuver, or manipulate spiritual energy. It is a matter of letting go and receiving what is given freely."[59] Nepo accurately summarizes this practice, writing:

> By trying to create, we are created. By trying to express, we are expressed. By trying to discover meaning, we become meaningful. So, the measure of great art can be understood, not so much by the beauty achieved in birthing a singular piece, but more by the transformation it births in us for the journey of creating it. It is not the thing created that renews us, but the creative act that restores us to our place in the Mystery.[60]

Thus, according to Nepo, "Over a lifetime, we experience an evolving sense of fitting things together, through which we are put together."[61] Rohr refers to this as looking at an object and suspending all other activity, being simply aware: "We relax into our basic awareness. We rest with the world as it is . . . . We are face to face with the calm . . . . We contemplate the object as it is. Great art has this power, this power to grab your attention and suspend it; we stare, sometimes awestruck, sometimes silent . . . ."[62] We are one with the created object and, consequently, transformed by the disciplined practice required by the journey to get to such glorious unity.

A third disciplined activity or practice is walking. Kagge says it is essential to human well-being. "You live longer," he states. "Your memory

---

57. Rohr, "An Uncreated Spark."
58. Rohr, "Fallow Time."
59. Rohr, "DNA."
60. Nepo, "Our Walk," 82.
61. Nepo, "Our Walk," 83.
62. Rohr, "Practice: Contemplating Art."

sharpens. Your blood pressure falls. Your immune system gets stronger."[63] While walking may be a slow undertaking, Kagge says, it is a radical thing to do, and, echoing the topic of creativity being a disciplined activity, he states, "[W]alking is a great tool for creativity."[64] Why? Because walking is a spiritual experience, according to Kagge. It is "a spiritual journey. You move your body, and you are being moved. People walk on pilgrimages—no one drives . . . . You can see the world, your fellow citizens, and yourself from a different angle."[65] Walking, as a spiritual discipline, is one of the building blocks employed today to erect Christian spirituality from the bottom-up. Poust calls walking an everyday moment, a pilgrim moment. It is "a path that can show [one] new ways to grow closer to Christ."[66]

Reflections

This book presents spiritual *reflections* for travelers. As a noun, the word, *reflections*, refers to expressing something in the hope that one will think seriously, carefully, and relatively calmly about it. The basis for the reflections is Scripture. Various biblical texts about journey, pilgrimage, path, trip, trail, etc. are presented for the reader's contemplation. The reflection provided for each entry uses the process outlined above: (1) order, (2) hearing the call to journey, (3) answering the call to journey by preparation, (4) entering the disordered chaos of taking the journey and being transformed, and (5) coming home reordered and transformed. The author gleans the spirituality from the biblical text in his reflective words, and then he invites you to make an application to your life; thus, you may grow in spirituality through your lifetime journey into God.

Biblical stories have been chosen because "spirituality is something worth exploring by getting to know the words and teachings of wise elders who came before us," states McColman.[67] And there is no other book full of the teachings of wise elders better than the Bible. Furthermore, "Much of the Bible takes place in movement, and this is no coincidence," writes Walsh. "For it instructs a path of faith that is always a letting go

63. Kagge, "Five Questions," 88.
64. Kagge, "Five Questions," 88.
65. Kagge, "Five Questions," 88.
66. Poust, *Everyday Divine*, 160.
67. McColman, *Answering*, 119.

Introduction

of locations, fixed spots, and emotional needs for a certain kind of God and moving toward something greater and freer...."[68] She adds, "Most of the [Hebrew Bible (Old Testament)] Torah takes place in transit, from slavery toward a freedom with God."[69] According to Wright, "[A]ll truth, whether divinely revealed or discovered by intellectual reflection on the world, is from God."[70] He adds, "[T]he various realities meditated by the biblical text are revelatory and salvific: In them is concealed and revealed the living God, who works in the course of the divine economy to bring about the salvation of the world."[71] Most importantly for our purposes here, Wright presents a spiritual understanding of biblical texts. He explains this as "a Spirit-conferred faith experience of the reality mediated by the sacred text, and a perception of how that reality shares in the mystery of the whole Christ," that is, the mystical union of Christ and the church. Thus, the spiritual understanding of a biblical text "is spiritual primarily because it comes from the Holy Spirit's work...."[72] By reading the Scriptures and reflections presented here and contemplating their words, the reader enters into meditation, "the inner process of reflecting on the wisdom" of wise elders who came before us.[73]

Living reflectively in grace, we continue our journey by making application of the wisdom learned. Hollis writes: "Life happens, and we are the only creatures who try to understand it, make sense of it, experience meaning from it.... So we create stories.... [W]e 'story' everything around us. [The] story gets fixed within us and then leads to behavioral patterns later in life...."[74] We can affirm, adjust, or change our stories through reflection upon the stories others told on their journey into God.

Travelers

This book presents spiritual reflections for *travelers*. A traveler is anyone on a journey of any kind. Thus, an ordinary trip to the grocery store is a

68. Walsh, *Chasing Mystery*, 80.
69. Walsh, *Chasing Mystery*, 81.
70. Wright, *Encountering*, 126.
71. Wright, *Encountering*, 201.
72. Wright, *Encountering*, 226.
73. McColman, *Answering*, 119.
74. Kiesling, "Personal Accountability," 49–50.

Introduction

journey worthy of spiritual reflection. A walk to and around a nearby park is a journey. A visit to a state or national park, a monument, or wilderness area is a journey. The person making the journey is a traveler.

The word *traveler* has many synonyms, which make it ideally broad for choosing biblical texts upon which to reflect. Above we explored walking—to which we will return later—as a spiritual practice; to that could be added the walkabout, an extended journey on foot in a remote country or in a remote area of a country. Some walkers are also runners and/or racers, and they need endurance (Heb 10:36) to "run with perseverance the race that is set before" them (Heb 12:1) in order to finish the race (2 Tim 4:7).

Another synonym for traveler is sojourner. A sojourn is a brief visit or stay at a place.[75] After leaving Canaan and journeying to Goshen in Egypt, Jacob is presented by his son, Joseph, to Pharaoh, and Jacob characterizes his life and the lives of his ancestors as one of sojourning: "The years of my earthly sojourn are one hundred thirty; few and hard have been the years of my life. They do not compare with the years of the life of my ancestors, during their long sojourn," a reference to Abraham's and Isaac's years in Canaan (Gen 47:9). The author of OT (A) book of Wisdom—at the time of its writing between the first century BCE and the second century CE—states that Jacob's ancestors "still recall the events of their sojourn" (Wis 19:10). The OT (A) book of First Esdras characterizes the Jews who returned to Jerusalem from Babylonian captivity as "the Judeans who came up out of their sojourn in exile" (1 Esd 5:7). The psalmist explains that "evil will not sojourn with [God]" because he does not delight in wickedness when he travels (Ps 5:4).

One of the most-used words to describe a traveler is *pilgrim*. A pilgrim is a religious traveler who goes on a journey—a pilgrimage—to a holy place for religious reasons. Paintner writes: "A pilgrimage is . . . a journey of discovery. We prepare ourselves for an encounter with the holy presence which will always evoke awe and trembling."[76] Every year many people make the five-hundred-mile pilgrimage—called the Camino de Compostela—on foot from Saint Jean-Pied-de-Port in France to Santiago de Compostela, Spain. Other people travel in a car on pilgrimage to a Marian shrine, like those in Lourdes, France; Fatima, Portugal; Czestochowa, Poland; or Guadalupe, Mexico. McColman reminds us that Chaucer, in *Canterbury Tales*,

---

75. Only four uses of sojourn are found in the New Revised Standard Version of the Bible.

76. Paintner, *Soul*, 85.

INTRODUCTION

"compares the human experience to a religious pilgrimage,"[77] as the various travelers make their way to the shrine of Saint Thomas Becket, who was murdered in Canterbury Cathedral. Other pilgrimage destinations include the Kaaba in Mecca, Saudi Arabia; the Western Wall in Jerusalem, Israel; the Basilica of Saint Peter in Vatican City, Italy; the Golden Temple in Amritsar, India; and Stonehenge outside Salisbury, England.

Flanagan reminds us that "the church is a pilgrim and not simply a wanderer."[78] The Roman Catholic bishops of Vatican Council II (1962–1965) referred to the church as "a pilgrim now on earth."[79] "The image of the pilgrim church," writes Flanagan,

> suggests how the church is always on a journey toward the fullness of grace, always participating in the fullness of the reign of God partially and in a preliminary way. And yet, the pilgrim church knows where God's promised land lies and the general direction toward which it is heading, even if the mystery of evil and sin, and God's respect of human freedom, allows not only for individuals to wander off that path, but for the community as a whole to sometimes stumble or take an extended detour.[80]

The church is best imaged as a group of pilgrims walking together towards God. Again, Flanagan explains the image of the church on its pilgrimage as

> the reality of the church's journey in the midst of eschatological tension, the bonds between those who walk on pilgrimage together, the dynamic between knowledge of the final destination and regular failure to follow the most direct path toward that destination, and the dependence of the church upon God, and especially upon God's Holy Spirit leading and guiding the church through the desert of our current wondering.[81]

Being a pilgrim on a journey is not a static state. According to Flanagan, we look "forward to the day and the place that we the pilgrim church have not yet reached, to the kingdom that has not yet come."[82] Flanagan's words echo those spoken by Uriel to Ezra in the OT (A): " . . . I will rejoice

77. McColman, *Answering*, xi.
78. Flanagan, *Stumbling*, 169.
79. "Dogmatic Constitution on the Church," par. 14; cf. pars. 48–51.
80. Flanagan, *Stumbling*, 176.
81. Flanagan, *Stumbling*, 177.
82. Flanagan, *Stumbling*, 178.

Introduction

over the creation of the righteous, over their pilgrimage also, and their salvation, and their receiving their reward" (2 Esd 8:39).[83] All the other travels we take, all the other paths we walk, all the other trails we follow are reminders that we individually and collectively are pilgrims on a journey into God.

Using This Book

This book is designed to be used by individuals for private study and prayer and by ministers for study, prayer, and preaching. The goal of this book is to foster the spirituality of journey as it flows from the Bible. Chapter 1 presents entries on journey. Chapter 2 is focused on the road one travels on a journey. Path is the subject of chapter 3, while route, highway, and gateway are presented in chapter 4. Chapter 5 presents entries on walking, and chapter 6 covers the way or route one travels. Chapter 7 serves as a summary, showing how the journey metaphor is present in *The Roman Missal*.

A five-part exercise is offered for the ninety-seven biblical entries divided into seven chapters.

1. **Title:** A short title is given to the entry. Not only does the title give focus to the entry, but it imitates *Lectio Divina* (Divine Reading), the practice of reading a biblical passage and choosing a word or two from it for reflection, meditation, and prayer. *Lectio Divina* promotes communion with God through reflection on God's Word (Jesus Christ)

---

83. This is the only time the word *pilgrimage* is used in any book in the New Revised Standard Version of the Bible.

Introduction

and God's word (Bible). Traditionally, *Lectio Divina* has four separate steps: read, reflect, journal/meditate, and pray or contemplate.

The title is designed to promote mindfulness. According to Annemarie Scobey:

> Mindfulness is the practice of maintaining a moment-by-moment awareness of thoughts, feelings, the body, and the surrounding environment. A person who tries to be mindful focuses on what he or she senses and feels in the present moment rather than thinking about what might need to be done later or returning to a memory. Mindfulness is the opposite of multitasking. Mindfulness is truly listening, fully tasting, deeply experiencing; it's taking our feelings as they come and not burying them or pushing them away.[84]

2. **Scripture**: Since the focus of the entry is found in the title, a verse or two from a Scripture passage illustrating the theme of the chapter is presented. Because of the difference in verse numbering between Bibles, as explained in "Notes on the Bible" below, alternate numbering indicating the Vulgate verse numbering is presented in parentheses and/or brackets when necessary.

While reading the biblical text, a word other than the one presented may get the reader's attention. In this case, the reader should follow the guidance of the Holy Spirit and use his or her word for the *Lectio Divina* process of reading, reflecting, journaling/meditating, and praying or contemplating.

3. **Reflection**: The Scripture passage is followed by a reflection on the biblical passage and its application to the theme of the chapter. Throughout the reflections, the masculine pronoun for God, LORD, LORD God, etc. is used. The author is well aware that God is neither male nor female, but in order to avoid the repetition of nouns over and over again, he employs male pronouns, as they are also used in most biblical translations.

4. **Meditation/Journal**: The reflection is followed by a question for personal meditation and/or journaling. The question functions as a guide for personal appropriation of the spiritual journey, thus leading the reader into personal prayer and/or journaling. The meditation/

---

84. Scobey, "Keep Prayer in Mind," 43.

Introduction

journal question is designed to foster a process of actively applying the reflection to one's life and further development of it. The question gets one started; where the meditation/journal goes cannot be predetermined. It may be a single statement or an idea with which one lingers for a few minutes, a few hours, or a few days. Such contemplation has no end; the reader decides when he or she has finished his or her exploration because he or she needs to attend to other things. People who like to journal—written or electronic—will find the question appropriate for that activity.

According to Scobey:

> Meditation involves quieting the mind and heart. It is a time of focusing our attention on a sacred word or on our breath; a time of letting our thoughts pass by, without holding onto them or entering into them. It is a time of deep awareness . . . . A common theme . . . is silence and stillness. Contemplation, a cousin of meditation, was explained by St. Gregory the Great in the sixth century as "resting in God." St. Gregory went on to explain that in this "resting," the mind and heart are not so much seeking God as beginning to experience God's actual presence. The reduction of action and thought, according to St. Gregory, allows the person practicing contemplation to sustain [his or her] consent to God's presence. In other words—without action and thought, less gets in the way of experiencing God.[85]

In *Rosarium Virginis Mariae*, Pope St. John Paul II states, "Listening and mediation are nourished by silence."[86] He continues: "A discovery of the importance of silence is one of the secrets of practicing contemplation and mediation. One drawback of a society dominated by technology and the mass media is the fact that silence becomes increasingly difficult to achieve . . . . [I]t is fitting to pause briefly after listening to the word of God, while the mind focuses on the content" of the biblical passage and the reflection.[87]

5. **Prayer:** A prayer concludes the exercise and summarizes the title, which was illustrated by the Scripture, explored in the reflection, and served as the foundation for the meditation/journal exercise.

---

85. Scobey, "Keep Prayer in Mind," 43–44.
86. "*Rosarium*," par. 31.
87. "*Rosarium*," par. 31.

Introduction

Through this process of prayer with the focus on the spirituality of journey, the reader will come to a deeper knowledge of and a closer relationship with God through the roads, paths, and trails upon which he or she travels.

Notes on the Bible

The Bible is divided into two parts: The Hebrew Bible (Old Testament) and the Christian Bible (New Testament). The Hebrew Bible consists of thirty-nine named books accepted by Jews and Protestants as Holy Scripture. The Old Testament also contains those thirty-nine books plus seven to fifteen more named books or parts of books called the Apocrypha or the Deuterocanonical Books; the Old Testament is accepted by Catholics and several other Christian denominations as Holy Scripture. The Christian Bible, consisting of twenty-seven named books, is also called the New Testament; it is accepted by Christians as Holy Scripture. Thus, in this work:

—Hebrew Bible (Old Testament), abbreviated HB (OT), indicates that a book is found both in the Hebrew Bible and the Old Testament;

—Old Testament (Apocrypha), abbreviated OT (A), indicates that a book is found only in the Old Testament Apocrypha and not in the Hebrew Bible;

—and Christian Bible (New Testament), abbreviated CB (NT), indicates that a book is found only in the Christian Bible or New Testament.

In notating biblical texts, the first number refers to the chapter in the book, and the second number refers to the verse within the chapter. Thus, HB (OT) Isa 7:11 means that the quotation comes from Isaiah, chapter 7, verse 11. OT (A) Sirach 39:30 means that the quotation comes from Sirach, chapter 39, verse 30. CB (NT) Mark 6:2 means that the quotation comes from Mark's Gospel, chapter 6, verse 2. When more than one sentence appears in a verse, the letters a, b, c, etc. indicate the sentence being referenced in the verse. Thus, HB (OT) 2 Kgs 1:6a means that the quotation comes from the Second Book of Kings, chapter 1, verse 6, sentence 1. Also, poetry, such as the Psalms and sections of Judith, Proverbs, and Isaiah, may be noted using the letters a, b, c, etc. to indicate the lines being used. Thus, Psalm 16:4a refers to the first line of verse 4 of Psalm 16; there are two more lines of verse 4: b and c.

Introduction

Because there may be a difference in the verse numbers between the New Revised Standard Version (NRSV) and the Vulgate (the Latin translation of the Septuagint, such as *The New American Bible Revised Edition* [NABRE]), alternative verse numbers appear in parentheses or brackets as necessary. This is true particularly with the Psalms, but with other books as well. Thus, NRSV Isaiah 9:2–7 is NABRE (Vulgate) Isaiah 9:1–6; NRSV Isaiah 9:2–4, 6–7 is NABRE (Vulgate) Isaiah 9:1–3, 5–6. Introductory material to Bibles usually indicates which verse-numbering is being used.

In the HB (OT) and the OT (A), the reader often sees LORD (note all capital letters). Because God's name (Yahweh or YHWH (or YHVH), referred to as the Tetragrammaton) is not to be pronounced, the name Adonai (meaning *Lord*) is substituted for Yahweh when a biblical text is read. When a biblical text is translated and printed, LORD (cf. Gen 2:4) is used to alert the reader to what the text actually states: Yahweh. Furthermore, when the biblical author writes Lord Yahweh, printers present Lord GOD (note all capital letters for GOD; cf. Gen 15:2) to avoid the printed ambiguity of LORD LORD. When the reference is to Jesus, the word printed is Lord (note capital L and lower case letters; cf. Luke 11:1). When writing about a lord (note all lower case letters (cf. Matt 18:25) with servants, no capital L is used.

Presuppositions

The HB (OT) begins as stories passed on by word of mouth from one person to another. Sometime during the oral transmission stage, authors decided to collect the oral stories and write them. A change occurs immediately. One does not tell a story the same way one writes a story. Repetition and correction occur in oral story-telling. Except for future emendations by copyists, single statements by characters and plot structure guides dominate written stories. Furthermore, in both oral and written story-telling, types or models are employed. In the HB (OT), for example, Joshua and Elijah are types of Moses. In the CB (NT) Elizabeth becomes a type of Hannah, who is herself a type of Sarah. When orally narrating or writing a story, the teller or author consciously creates one character as a type of another in order to make the character and his or her words and actions intelligible to the hearer or reader.

Introduction

In the CB (NT) the oldest gospel is Mark's account of Jesus' victory. The author of Matthew's Gospel copied and shortened about eighty percent of Mark's material into his book and then added other stories to make the work longer. The author of Luke's Gospel copied and shortened about fifty percent of Mark's material into his orderly account and then added other stories to make the work much longer. Mark's Gospel begins as oral story-telling, lasting for about forty years in that form. An unidentified author, called Mark for the sake of convenience, collects the oral stories, sets a plot, and writes the first gospel around 70 CE. Because Jesus was expected to return soon, no one had thought about recording what he had said and done until Mark came along and realized that he was not returning as quickly as had been thought. About ten years after Mark finished his gospel, Matthew needed to adopt Mark's narrative—originally intended for a peasant Gentile readership—to a Jewish audience. And about twenty years after Mark finished his gospel, Luke needed to adapt Mark's poor Gentile-intended work for a rich, upper class, urban, Gentile readership. The author of John's Gospel did not know the existence of the other three works collectively named synoptic gospels.

Furthermore, gospels were not first intended to be read privately as is done today. They were meant to be heard in a group. The very low rate of literacy in the first century would have never dictated many copies of texts since most people could not read, and their standard practice was to listen to another read the stories to them. Thus, what began as oral story-telling passed on by word of mouth became written story-telling preserved in gospels. A careful reading of Mark's Gospel will reveal the orality still embedded in the text, especially evident in the repetition of words and the organization of stories in three parts. In rewriting Mark, Matthew and Luke remove the last traces of oral story-telling.

Let's now begin with an exercise from the book of the prophet Ezekiel.

Ezekiel's Baggage

Scripture: "The word of the LORD came to me: . . . [M]ortal, prepare for yourself an exile's baggage, and go into exile by day in [the house of Israel's] sight; you shall go like an exile from your place to another place in their sight. You shall bring out your baggage by day in their sight, as baggage for exile; and you shall go out yourself at evening in their sight, as those do who go into exile. Dig through the wall in their sight, and carry the baggage through it. In their sight you shall lift the baggage on your shoulder, and carry it out in the dark; you shall cover your face, so that you may not see the land; for I have made you a sign for the house of Israel." (Ezek 12:1, 3–6)

Reflection: A sign is a thing or person that points toward another thing or person. In the HB (OT) book of Ezekiel, God makes his prophet enact the sign by packing his suitcase as if he were going on a journey into exile; this means that he will have a very small bag to carry on his way from Jerusalem to Babylon. God instructs Ezekiel to carry his suitcase both during the day and during the evening on his shoulder. After digging a hole in the wall, he is to pass through it with his baggage. He is a sign of the exile that awaits the people of Jerusalem to Babylon.

You are getting ready to take a trip, a spiritual journey. Every one of us spends anywhere from a few days to maybe a hundred years or more on the planet that makes a complete elliptical journey around the sun approximately every 365.24 days. Others have done this before; they came into existence, they journeyed for years, and then they returned to the dust out of which they were made (Gen 3:19). Eventually, Ezekiel journeys with his fellow Jews from Jerusalem to Babylon. By examining his trip—and others like it found in the Bible—we may get a little help, insight, or guidance for our own. This, like other reflections in this book, is presented as an aid on the journey. Such biblical passages do not exhaust the theme of spiritual journey; they and their reflections are chosen for their ability to deepen your understanding of spiritual travel. So, pack your spiritual suitcase and get ready for a trip that can transform your life.

Meditation/Journal: While looking at a piece of your luggage, ask yourself: What memories does this baggage contain of travel? How does it remind me that I am on a journey into God? How is God seeking expression in the world through my spiritual journey?

Prayer: LORD, God of Ezekiel, you made your prophet a sign to your people. Make me a sign of the journey into you. Guide my steps through spiritual travel that I may not end in exile, but in your divine presence. All praise be to you, Father, Son, and Holy Spirit, one God, forever and ever. Amen.

1

Journey

Abram and Sarai

Scripture: "Now the LORD said to Abram, 'Go from your country and your kindred and your father's house to the land that I will show you.' So Abram went, as the LORD had told him.... Abram took his wife Sarai... and all the possessions that they had gathered...; and they set forth to go to the land of Canaan. When they had come to the land of Canaan, Abram passed through the land to the place at Shechem, to the oak of Moreh. Then the

LORD appeared to Abram, and said, 'To your offspring I will give this land.' So he built there an altar to the LORD, who had appeared to him. From there he moved on to the hill country on the east of Bethel, and pitched his tent . . . ; and there he built an altar to the LORD and invoked the name of the LORD. And Abram journeyed on by stages toward the Negeb." (Gen 12:1, 4a, 5–6a, 7–9)

Reflection: Abram and Sarai continue a journey to Canaan (modern day Lebanon, Syria, Jordan, and Israel) that began with Abram's father, Terah, who left the town of Ur in Chaldea (Babylon) and settled in Haran (Gen 11:31). In Haran, Abram and Sarai are living an ordered and prosperous life when they hear the LORD's call to continue the journey to Canaan. They answer by gathering and packing all their possessions—indicating they have no intention to return—and traveling to Shechem, where they pitch their tent under an oak tree, sometimes called a terebinth. An oak tree represents strength, might, endurance, longevity, and nobility, characteristics of Abram and Sarai. As a sacred place, in biblical literature important events take place under an oak tree.[1] In this narrative, God appears to Abram and promises to give the land to his descendants; this is rather outrageous because Sarai was barren (Gen 11:30); Abram has no descendants! Nevertheless, Abram responds by building an altar to the LORD—in two places to signify the divine presence[2]—and calling him his God. The One who called the patriarch and his wife to take the journey is trustworthy. Then, Abram and Sarai continue their journey south into a hot, dry region known as the Negeb.

You (and your spouse) are most likely living comfortably in a multi-room home with at least one car—and probably two—in the driveway. (Both of) you have a daily, ordered schedule of awakening, eating breakfast, leaving home, going to work, breaking for lunch, more work, going home, preparing dinner, relaxing, and going to bed. If you heard the voice of God calling you to leave all that you have built behind and head off to South America or Africa, would you make the journey? In other words, would you be willing to leave order and enter into chaos for a long period of time? The HB (OT) book of Genesis continues the narrative about Abram and Sarai (Gen 12:10—25:11) focusing on the transformation that takes place in

---

1. For more on the significance of oak trees, see *An Abecedarian of Sacred Trees* by Mark G. Boyer (Eugene, OR: Wipf and Stock, 2016) 106–111.

2. For more on the significance of altars, see *Divine Presence: Elements of Biblical Theophanies* by Mark G. Boyer (Eugene, OR: Wipf and Stock, 2017) 96–101.

that couple—even their names were changed to Abraham and Sarah—who left their ordered life of Haran after hearing a call from God to journey to Canaan and elsewhere.

Meditation/Journal: What journey have you made with all your possessions? Who (What) called you to move? Where did you go? Was God behind the call? What kind of altar did you build in honor of the divine presence? Explain.

Prayer: LORD, just as you have called and appeared to Abram and Sarai, so you have called and appeared to me on my lifetime journey. Everywhere are altars—tables, oak trees, roads—signifying your presence. Bring me home to you transformed to live with you and Abram and Sarai forever. Amen.

Joseph's Family

Scripture: "Pharaoh said to Joseph, 'Say to your brothers, "Take your father and your households and come to me, so that I may give you the best of the land of Egypt, and you may enjoy the fat of the land." You are further charged to say, "Do this: take wagons from the land of Egypt for your little ones and for your wives, and bring your father, and come. Give no thought to your possessions, for the best of all the land of Egypt is yours."' So they went up out of Egypt and came to their father Jacob in the land of Canaan. And they told him, 'Joseph is still alive!' Israel said, 'I must go and see him before I die.' When Israel set out on his journey with all that he had . . . , he offered sacrifices to the God of his father Isaac. God spoke to Israel in visions of the night, and said, 'Jacob, Jacob.' And he said, 'Here I am.' Then he said, 'I am God, the God of your father; do not be afraid to go down to Egypt, for I will make of you a great nation there. I myself will go down with you to Egypt, and I will also bring you up again . . . .'" (Gen 45:17–20, 25–26a, 28ac; 46:1–4)

Reflection: The novelette concerning the exploits of Joseph, son of Jacob (also known as Israel), occupies chapter 37 through chapter 50 of the book of Genesis; it is the longest continuous narrative in the book. Most people know the story about Joseph being sold into slavery by his brothers and rising to power in Egypt, after which his boss, Pharaoh, tells Joseph to invite his father, Jacob, and his eleven brothers to come to Egypt to avoid the famine that has occurred in Canaan. Jacob, son of Isaac, son of Abraham, has settled in Canaan and leads an orderly life there. After learning that the son he thought was dead is still alive, he decides to make the journey into disorder with his sons and daughters-in-law and grandchildren (Gen 46:7) and "their livestock and the goods that they had acquired in Canaan" (Gen 46:6) to settle in Goshen, Egypt. Not only is Jacob transformed by the news that Joseph is alive, but he becomes the agent of transformation for the rest of his family, which he uproots and moves to a land where there is food and water. However, it is Joseph who is the model for this novelette. He is sold into slavery (disorder), and then he is rescued by Pharaoh (order). His brothers and their descendants will become slaves (disorder) and be rescued by Moses (order). Both Pharaoh and Moses are instruments of the God who speaks to Jacob during the night.

The liminal space that Joseph and Jacob have entered in Egypt is where the transformation occurs. This move is a type of a rite of passage. In Egypt, the Hebrews will regenerate and become a great nation through their journey on the rough road of slavery. Barr writes: "A liminal space is a place of transition, one where we often feel unsettled or anxious. Life is not as it was before, but we don't yet know how it's going to be."[3] This is exactly the spot Joseph and Jacob occupy. They need faith in the God of Abraham and Isaac. In the words of Hudson, they need a faith that "arises out of a deeper trust in spirit, in God." He continues: "As we take a journey into faith, it is of necessity a journey into liminal space. It takes us beyond our old beliefs into new discoveries about ourselves, our relationships, and the nature of God."[4] The sojourn in Egypt is a spiritual journey beyond the Hebrews' familiar world. There they "learn to live in a condition of continual awakening, continual shifts of awareness, and deepening mystery." They "learn to live more in a state of liminality."[5] After redefining liminality, Danaher summarizes what occurs to the next generation of Hebrews following Jacob and Joseph in liminal space:

> Liminality refers to that transitional space between what was and what is next. Liminal space is where all transformation takes place and is an essential element of the deeper truth to which God is always calling us.... [T]ransformative liminal space... ushers us into a radically different perspective and radically different way to

---

3. Barr, "A Meditation," 36.
4. Hudson, "Liminality," 75.
5. Hudson, "Liminality," 70.

be.... We have to stop identifying with who we are in this world and start identifying with who we are in God.⁶

And that is exactly what the Hebrews do in preparation for God to send Moses to lead them out of Egypt and back to Canaan.

Meditation/Journal: What experience of liminal space brought you to stop identifying with who you are in this world and begin identifying with who you are in God?

Prayer: Protect me, Mighty One of Jacob. Guide me on my journey, O Shepherd and Rock of Israel. Bless me, Almighty, with graces from heaven that enable me to walk through transformation to renewed life in you. Amen.

Moses

Scripture: "God said to Moses, 'Go and assemble the elders of Israel.... They will listen to your voice; and you and the elders of Israel shall go to the king of Egypt and say to him, "The LORD, the God of the Hebrews, has met with us; let us now go a three days' journey into the wilderness, so that we may sacrifice to the LORD our God."' Moses said to Pharaoh, 'We must go a three days' journey into the wilderness and sacrifice to the LORD our God as he commands us.'... Moses... went to Pharaoh and said, 'Thus says the LORD, the God of Israel, "Let my people go, so that they may celebrate a festival to me in the wilderness."' But Pharaoh said, 'Who is the LORD, that I should heed him and let Israel go? I do not know the LORD, and I will not let Israel go.' Then [Moses] said, 'The God of the Hebrews has revealed himself to us; let us go a three days' journey into the wilderness to sacrifice to the LORD our God.... We must go a three days' journey into the wilderness and sacrifice to the LORD our God as he commands us.'" (Exod 3:14a, 16a, 18; 5:1–3; 8:27)

Reflection: Before the exodus occurs, God tells Moses to seek permission from Pharaoh to go on a three-day journey into the wilderness in order to sacrifice to the LORD. As can be seen above, the request for a three-day journey into the wilderness is repeated over and over again. In biblical numerology, three is a sacred number referring not to quantity, but to quality. In other words, three is the number for the divine—even before the

---

6. Danher, "Truth," 63–4.

doctrine of the Trinity is established! As a reference to the spiritual world, it gives a sense of order to the chaos of the lives of the Hebrew slaves. Furthermore, it generates a sense of expectation; something new and exciting—a transformation—is to occur.[7] The Hebrews are God's people, chosen to live a spiritual life, which, according to Robertson, "is about movement and evolution. Every moment, we stand on a new threshold, with its invitation to step into the tension and be stretched in frightening and exhilarating ways."[8] The Hebrews and Pharaoh are presented with a threshold, "the moment of liminal space between that which once was and what is to come."[9] The Hebrews are ready to enter it; Pharaoh is not.

The sacrifice to the LORD cannot be made on the foreign soil of Egypt. It must be made in the wilderness, where, biblically, God prefers to reveal himself to people. The LORD is found in the three-day trip led by Moses to an orderly sacrifice in the wilderness. The Hebrews view this journey to be one that takes them out of the chaos of slavery and into the order of the divine presence. Pharaoh views this journey to be one that takes the Hebrews out of the order of slavery and sets them free under the order of a God he does not know. As Robertson makes so clear above, daily we stand on thresholds—not as dramatically as Moses, Pharaoh, and the Hebrews—with the invitation to step into the unknown, the liminal, where we will be transformed. If we notice a set of three around—like three books, three people, three requests, three days, etc.—we should recognize the divine presence calling us out of chaos to order. Know that the LORD is found in the three-day trip!

Meditation/Journal: What liminal threshold have you recently crossed? What order did you leave behind to cross into disorder? What transformation occurred as you emerged into a reordered life?

Prayer: I sing to you, O LORD, for you triumph gloriously with your divine presence. Give me strength and might to journey across thresholds of transformation that become my spiritual salvation. You are my God, and I praise you and exalt you forever. Amen.

---

7. For more on the significance of sacred numbers, see *Divine Presence: Elements of Biblical Theophanies* by Mark G. Boyer (Eugene, OR: Wipf and Stock, 2017) 10-25.

8. Robertson, "On the Threshold," 60.

9. Robertson, "On the Threshold," 59.

Journey

Stages

Scripture: "The Israelites journeyed from Rameses to Succoth, about six hundred thousand men on foot, besides children. From the wilderness of Sin the whole congregation of the Israelites journeyed by stages, as the LORD commanded. On the third new moon after the Israelites had gone out of the land of Egypt, on that very day, they came into the wilderness of Sinai. They had journeyed from Rephidim, entered the wilderness of Sinai, and camped in the wilderness; Israel camped there in front of [Mount Sinai (Horeb)]." (Exod 12:37; 17:1a; 19:1-2)

Reflection: The Israelites journey in stages, periods during their process of getting from Egypt to Canaan. The four verses above from the HB (OT) book of Exodus present some of the stages or places they stopped to pitch camp for a period of time before breaking camp and moving on to the next stage of their journey. As Moses recounts in the HB (OT) book of Deuteronomy, it was the LORD who said to him, "Get up, go on your journey at the head of the people, that they may go in and occupy the land that I swore to their ancestors to give them" (Deut 10:11). For a fuller understanding of the stages of the journey, read Exodus 12:29-37; 13:17—19:1; and Numbers 10:11—22:1. There is also a summary of the stages in Numbers 33:1-54. As they journey by stages, they celebrate the Passover, the major event which pushed Pharaoh to set them free to leave Egypt (Exod 12:1-32; Num 9:1-5). They carry the ark, which God instructed them to make (Exod 25:1—31:18), along with all the other accoutrements that go with it. According to Numbers, the ark leads them (Num 10:33-36). They eat quail (Exod 16:13; Num 11:31-32) and manna (Exod 16:14-21). Stage by stage they made their way to Canaan led by the LORD, who appeared as a cloud over the tent of meeting in which was placed the ark (Exod 40:34-36).

While the stages of Israel's journey differ greatly from the stages of a modern journey, there are, nevertheless, comparisons to be made. We begin most trips by thinking about them and discussing them with our intended travel companion over dinner. The passover occurs when we reach a decision; we pass over from ideas to a plan to take a trip. In order to get out of town, we need to make arrangements with a tour company, travel agency, and/or an airline; an envelope full of tickets is required as well as a passport! We need to pack a bag or two—or three—of clothing, shoes, prescription drugs, and toiletries we will need while we are gone. Our leader is the captain, the cruise director, the tour guide, and/or the coach driver. Our unity as a family, as travel companions, and as a whole group gets celebrated with a few included meals at restaurants during the journey. The leader dresses in an easily-recognized uniform, carries an umbrella or unique object on a pole, or speaks to people on a specific channel through battery-powered headphones. Stage by stage we prepare to leave; we leave, and stage by stage we travel to our destination; stage by stage we make the trip no matter how long it takes; stage by stage we make our way home. We are transformed.

Meditation/Journal: What were the major stages of the last trip you took? What have been the major stages of your lifetime sacred journey?

Prayer: Your glory, O LORD, filled the tabernacle and covered the tent of meeting which led your people on their journey to the land you promised them. Reveal yourself to me at each stage of my journey and lead me to share the eternal light of your presence forever. Amen.

Joshua

Scripture: "After the death of Moses the servant of the LORD, the LORD spoke to Joshua son of Nun, Moses' assistant, saying, 'My servant Moses is dead. Now proceed to cross the Jordan, you and all this people, into the land that I am giving to them, to the Israelites. You are the one who shall command the priests who bear the ark of the covenant, "When you come to the edge of the waters of the Jordan, you shall stand still in the Jordan."' Joshua said, 'When the soles of the feet of the priests who bear the ark of the LORD, the Lord of all the earth, rest in the waters of the Jordan, the waters of the Jordan flowing from above shall be cut off; they shall stand in a single heap.' So when those who bore the ark had come to the Jordan, and the feet of the priests bearing the ark were dipped in the edge of the water, the waters flowing from above stood still, rising up in a single heap . . . . Then the people crossed over . . . . While all Israel were crossing over on dry ground, the priests who bore the ark of the covenant of the LORD stood on dry ground in the middle of the Jordan, until the entire nation finished crossing over the Jordan." (Josh 1:1–2; 3:8, 13, 15b–17)

Reflection: The final stage of Israel's journey is led by Joshua, whose name means "Yahweh is salvation." The meaning of his name refers to the LORD's act of saving his people from Pharaoh and his Egyptian army by parting the waters of the Red Sea, getting his people to the other side, and drowning the army in the waters (Exod 14:21–29). The narrator of the book of Exodus explains: "Thus the LORD saved Israel that day from the Egyptians. Israel saw the great work that the LORD did against the Egyptians" (Exod 14:30a, 31a). The author of the book of Joshua uses Moses as a model for Joshua, who, as the new leader and commander of the Israelites and the priests, is the means for God to save Israel again by crossing the Jordan River. Furthermore, this crossing of the Jordan under Joshua's leadership and the salvation of the Israelites is a prelude to all the battles from which the LORD will save Israel as the people conquer the inhabitants of the land of Canaan. When the soles of the feet of the priests bearing the ark touch the water, it stops flowing, just like the Red Sea parted when Moses extended his hands and staff over it. This is the culmination of the spiritual journey that has taken Israel forty years to finish; in other words, it is a lifetime journey. By crossing the Jordan in the same way they crossed the Red Sea—dry shod—the Israelites finish in the same way they began (Josh 4:23–24). And, once across, they must begin again!

Until we take our very last breath, we are always on a spiritual journey. The reordered end of the journey with the accompanied transformation sparked by the trip in the first place lasts only a short time before the next pilgrimage is begun. While we would like to stay put for a while, that is not possible for people on a spiritual journey of salvation. We hear the divine call. We know we must get busy and plan the next trip, enter into chaos and the ensuing transformation it brings before returning home with reordered lives. The soles of our feet are not glued to the dry earth; they are constantly moving in exploration, crossing boundary after boundary, maybe even stopping the flow of rivers, until we reach the land God promised.

Meditation/Journal: From what journey did you return transformed and know that you needed to begin quickly to plan the next trip? What call did you hear? To where did you pilgrimage next?

Prayer: I draw near to hear your word, O LORD of all the earth, that calls me to the next stage of my journey across the water. Guide my feet in your paths so that all may know that your hand is mighty to save now and forever. Amen.

Elijah

Scripture: " . . . [Elijah] went a day's journey into the wilderness, and came and sat down under a solitary broom tree. Then he lay down under the broom tree and fell asleep. The angel of the LORD came . . . , touched him, and said, 'Get up and eat, otherwise the journey will be too much for you.' He got up, and ate [a cake baked on hot stones] and drank [from a jar of water]; then he went in the strength of that food forty days and forty nights to Horeb the mount of God. At that place he came to a cave, and spent the night there. Then the word of the LORD came to him . . . ." (1 Kgs 19:4a, 5a, 7–9)

Reflection: The First and Second Book of Kings contain the narrative about the prophet Elijah (1 Kgs 17:1—2 Kgs 2:18). Elijah, whose name means "Yahweh is (my) God," is another HB (OT) character modeled on Moses. This is particularly noted because he travels to Mount Horeb (Sinai), the same mountain upon which Moses received the Torah, to seek direction from Yahweh, his God, for the next step of his lifetime journey. Before this the prophet has stopped the rain in Israel; traveled to Zarephath, where he was fed by a widow, whose son he raised from the dead; engaged in and won a trial by fire on Mount Carmel with the prophets of Baal; made it rain; and walked to Horeb.[10] He is tired of being the LORD's prophet; before he begins his journey to the holy mountain, he asks God to take his life (1 Kgs 19:4). Once he gets to Horeb (Sinai), he reminds God of his zeal for him and how his people want to kill him (1 Kgs 19:10). God sends him out of the cave—a type of womb in which Elijah has found order and security—to stand on the mountain—a place of chaos—to hear the LORD's voice directing his next step. Chaos reigns on the mountain: " . . . [T]here was a great wind, so strong that it was splitting mountains and breaking rocks in pieces before the LORD, but the LORD was not in the wind; and after the wind an earthquake, but the LORD was not in the earthquake; and after the earthquake a fire, but the Lord was not in the fire; and after the fire a sound of sheer silence" (1 Kgs 19:11b–12). It is in the sheer silence that he hears the call to continue his journey, and God gives him specific directions as to what he is to do now.

---

10. For more on Elijah, see *From Contemplation to Action: The Spiritual Process of Divine Discernment Using Elijah and Elisha as Models* by Mark G. Boyer (Eugene, OR: Wipf and Stock, 2018).

Journey

In our very ordered lives, all of us reach a point where we are tired, we need a break, a vacation, time off, a sabbatical, a promotion, etc. While we are comfortable in our man caves or she sheds, there is a restlessness that invades our work, play, relationships, prayer, etc. We may not have the luxury of retreating for a few days to a hermitage in the woods, but we can stop in some sheer silence in our bedroom or on a walk in the woods to hear the call from God to step out of our comfort zone and into the chaos and hear his voice of direction. Usually, the LORD calls us to take a journey, literally or figuratively. Literally, he may call us to a mission trip, a food-distribution center, a blood drive, etc. Figuratively, he may call us to a book to read, a class to take, a neighbor to help, etc. If we enter the chaos of the liminal moment—that is, take the journey—we will be transformed. Remember, while he was walking, "a chariot of fire and horses of fire [appeared], and Elijah ascended in a whirlwind into heaven" (2 Kgs 2:11). In other words, Elijah finished the life the LORD gave him to live and took him transformed on his last journey.

Meditation/Journal: When have you felt restless in your ordered life? What call did you hear? How did you answer it? What journey did you take? How were you transformed?

Prayer: O LORD, answer me. In sheer silence, call me out of my restlessness to a renewed zealousness for life, and give me the strength to journey into chaos that I might grow in your sight, O God of hosts. Direct my steps into transformation, as I continue to walk to you all the days of my life. Amen.

Tobias

Scripture: "[Tobias] . . . found the angel Raphael standing in front of him, but he did not perceive that he was an angel of God. Then Tobias said to him, 'Do you know the way to go to Media?' 'Yes,' he replied, 'I have been there many times; I am acquainted with it and know all the roads. It is a journey of two days . . . .' . . . So Tobias went in to tell his father Tobit and said to him, 'I have just found a man who is one of our own Israelite kindred!' He replied, 'Call the man in, my son, so that I may learn . . . whether he is trustworthy enough to go with you.' Then Tobias went out and called him . . . . So he went in to him, and Tobit greeted him . . . . Then Tobit said to him, '. . . [G]o with my son . . . .' Raphael answered, 'I will go with him;

so do not fear.' Then [Tobit] called his son and said to him, 'Son, prepare supplies for the journey and set out with your brother. May God in heaven bring you safely there and return you in good health to me; and may his angel, my son, accompany you both for your safety.' Before he went out to start his journey, he kissed his father and mother. Tobit then said to him, 'Have a safe journey.' The young man went out and the angel with him; and the dog came out with him and went along with them." (Tob 5:4b, 5c–6ac, 9, 10ab, 11a, 15b, 16b, 17bcde; 6:1b–2a)

Reflection: The OT (A) book of Tobit is a fourteen-chapter novella about a man named Tobit, who has a son named Tobias, who is sent on a journey to retrieve money—ten talents of silver (Tob 4:20)—that Tobit left in trust with a man in Media (Tob 4:1). Because Tobias does not know the man who has the money nor the way to Media, Tobias tells Tobit to find a trustworthy man to accompany him on the two-day journey to retrieve the funds. The journey sets in motion several events of the story: travel, adventure, demons, angels, magic, and love. Our focus here is on the preparation for the journey. Tobias finds the angel Raphael, whose name means "God heals," disguised as Azariah (Tob 5:13). Among his many other functions, Raphael is responsible for guarding Tobias on the trip to and from Media. When Tobit asks God to accompany Azariah and Tobias on their trip and keep them safe, he does not know that Azariah is Raphael in disguise. In turn, an angel, whether named or not, is God in disguise.[11] Thus, the novella is about God, who heals using the gall, heart, and liver of a fish who jumps out of the Tigris River and tries to swallow Tobias's foot (Tob 6:3–5) all the while directing the journey. And not to be forgotten is the dog, a faithful traveling companion on the quest.

As anyone who has ever traveled with another knows, it is important to pick the right traveling companion. Such a person may be a spouse or a good friend. Whoever he or she is, compatibility is required. The relationship on the journey must be harmonious, as two people exist and live together in the same room without conflict. If both traveling companions are compatible, both may declare the other to be an angel in disguise. If, however, they are not compatible, both may declare the other to be a demon in disguise, and, according to Raphael, need to burn the fish's heart and liver to make a smoke to drive away the evil spirit (Tob 6:8), as does Tobias on his wedding night with Sarah (Tob 8:2), in order not to end up dead like

---

11. For more on angels, see *A Month-by-Month Guide to Entertaining Angels* by Mark G. Boyer (Chicago, IL: ACTA, 1995).

her previous seven husbands (Tob 7:11). After accomplishing everything of his mission, even marriage, Tobias, Sarah, and Raphael return to Tobias's father. "And the dog went along behind them" (Tob 11:4b). Tobias finds his father in the courtyard, smears the fish's gall on his father's eyes, his cataracts fall off, and he can see. "So Tobit went in rejoicing and praising God at the top of his voice. Tobias reported to his father that his journey had been successful, that he had brought the money, [and] that he had married Raguel's daughter Sarah . . . " (Tob 11:15cd). Raphael fulfills the meaning of his name: God heals Tobit and Sarah and brings back Tobias to his parents.

Meditation/Journal: With whom have your traveled? Was he or she an angel or a demon in disguise? Can a dog be God in disguise? Explain.

Prayer: "Blessed be God, and blessed be his great name, and blessed be all his holy angels. May his holy name be blessed throughout all the ages. Exalt him in the presence of every living being, because he is our Lord and he is our God; he is our Father and he is God forever" (Tob 11:14bc; 13:4b). Amen.

Travel Light

Scripture: " . . . [Jesus] went about among the villages teaching. He called the twelve and began to send them out two by two, and gave them authority over the unclean spirits. He ordered them to take nothing for their journey except a staff; no bread, no bag, no money in their belts; but to wear sandals and not to put on two tunics. He said to them, 'Wherever you enter a house, stay there until you leave the place. If any place will not welcome you and they refuse to hear you, as you leave, shake off the dust that is on your feet as a testimony against them.' So they went out and proclaimed that all should repent. They cast out many demons, and anointed with oil many who were sick and cured them." (Mark 6:6b–13)

Reflection: Jesus is a traveler; he leaves his traditional hometown of Nazareth to journey among the villages outside of it and to teach those who are teachable. While doing this, he sends members of the twelve apostles (Mark 3:13–19) two by two with the "authority to cast out demons" (Mark 3:15) or unclean spirits, which, in Mark's Gospel, have the role of identifying Jesus as the Son of God (Mark 3:11; 5:7). The mission the twelve are empowered to perform on their two-by-two travels—casting out demons—both imitates and continues the mission of Jesus in Mark's Gospel; it is best understood today as healing (Mark 1:32–34, 39; 3:22; 5:2, 15–16, 18; 7:26, 29–30). Do not think of casting out demons or unclean spirits as exorcisms in horror movies; think about doctors, physician assistants, and nurses who heal diseases and sicknesses. Anyone, according to Mark's Gospel, can cast out a demon or heal (Mark 9:38–40). Matthew's version of this account links the authority Jesus gives to the twelve to cast out unclean spirits to curing every disease and every sickness (Matt 10:1), as does Luke's version (Luke 9:1). When we say, "Bless you," after someone sneezes, in terms of the ancient world's belief that unclean spirits inhabit people and one has just been expelled through the sneeze, we are praising God for casting out an unclean spirit or demon!

Putting demons and unclean spirits aside, we move on to the apostolic journey which requires nothing except a walking stick, sandals, and the one set of clothes worn by an apostle. In other words, the twelve are instructed to travel light. Both the author of Matthew's Gospel and the author of Luke's Gospel permit the twelve disciples to travel even lighter than Mark does; they cannot bring anything, except, of course, the clothes they wear (Matt 10:9–10; Luke 9:3; 10:4). The message presented by the stories is that it is easy to get bogged down with stuff! No one of us would even begin to entertain the ideal of taking a trip without a suitcase full of clothes and a carry-on bag with medicines, toiletries, and other things inside. But there may be other containers with which we make our lifetime journey, like collections of collectibles (coins, plates, stamps, crystal, etc.); like psychological baggage of sword-hurting words, dagger-wounding experiences, divorces, being fired from a job, etc.; like spiritually receiving no answer to our prayers, petitions, devotions, etc. If we suddenly discover that we haul around any such baggage, we need the help of a mental health professional to repent, or for a physical ailment we need a medical team to cast out demons and unclean spirits by anointing us with antiseptic salve and writing a prescription for healing drugs. According to Rohr, " . . . [A]uthentic spirituality is not about getting, attaining, achieving, performing, or succeeding. . . . It is much more about letting go—letting go of what we don't need anyway . . . ."[12]

---

12. Rohr, "Less is More."

Meditation/Journal: As you make your lifetime journey on earth, what baggage slows you? What unclean spirit or demon needs to be cast out? What keeps you from traveling light?

Prayer: I thank you, Father, Lord of heaven and earth, because you have called me to journey unhindered to you. Guide my steps in those of your Son, who has revealed the way to you. Fill me with the breath of the Holy Spirit today, tomorrow, and forever. Amen.

Jesus' Journey

Scripture: "When the time came for [Jesus' parents'] purification according to the law of Moses, they brought him up to Jerusalem to present him to the Lord, (as it is written in the law of the Lord, 'Every firstborn male shall be designated as holy to the Lord'), and they offered a sacrifice according to what is stated in the law of the Lord, 'A pair turtledoves or two young pigeons.' Now every year his parents went to Jerusalem for the festival of the Passover. And when he was twelve years old, they went up as usual for the festival." (Luke 2:22–24, 41–42)

Reflection: The author of Luke's Gospel presents Jesus as a man on a journey. After he is conceived in the womb of his mother, Mary, they go with haste to the hill country to visit Zechariah and Elizabeth, and they stay there for about three months (Luke 1:26–56). Then they journey to Bethlehem to be registered; while in Bethlehem, Jesus is born (Luke 2:1–7). Eight days later, Joseph and Mary bring Jesus to Jerusalem (Luke 2:21–24), and twelve years later they again journey to Jerusalem for Passover (Luke 2:41–52). Thus, in the first two chapters of Luke's Gospel, Jesus is presented as a journeyer even while still in the womb! Even the rest of Luke's Gospel is built around Jesus traveling to Jerusalem. "When the days drew near for him to be taken up, he set his face to go to Jerusalem," writes Luke (9:51). That motif continues until 19:28, where Luke writes, " . . . [H]e went on ahead, going up to Jerusalem."

Biblical scholars label Luke 9:51—19:28 the journey to Jerusalem section of the gospel. By the time the third gospel was written, around 90 CE, the Christian life was being imaged as a journey from conception to death. Before Jesus begins his trip, he tells his disciples that "he must undergo great suffering, and be rejected by the elders, chief priests, and scribes, and be killed, and on the third day be raised" (Luke 9:22); he "is going to be betrayed into human hands" (Luke 9:44). Sprinkled throughout the journey to Jerusalem chapters are more of Jesus' words about his suffering and death. He states, " . . . [T]oday, tomorrow, and the next day I must be on my way, because it is impossible for a prophet to be killed outside of Jerusalem" (Luke 13:33). Later, speaking to the twelve, he explains that "he will be handed over to the Gentiles; and he will be mocked and insulted and spat upon. After they have flogged him, they will kill him, and on the third day he will rise again" (Luke 18:32–33). The author of this gospel finishes his message about the Christian life being one of following Jesus by portraying Simon of Cyrene carrying the cross behind Jesus (Luke 23:26). After Jesus dies on that cross, he is laid in a tomb, from which he is raised three days later (Luke 23:32—24:49). Even after he is raised from the dead, the Lukan Jesus continues to teach his disciples that the Christian life is a journey from conception to death (Luke 24:26–27, 44–47). Those who claim the name Christian need to be on a journey of always dying and rising.

Meditation/Journal: How is your sacred journey characterized by dying and rising? Make a list of the specific occasions or years when this occurred. How do these experiences give you hope for life after final death?

Prayer: Creator God, from conception to death you call me to journey in the footsteps of Jesus, your Son. Give me the strength of the Holy Spirit to be faithful to my mission that I may one day arrive at eternal life in your kingdom and praise you forever. Amen.

Peter and Paul

Scripture: " . . . [Cornelius] called two of his slaves and a devout soldier from the ranks of those who served him, and after telling them everything [about his vision of an angel of God], he sent them to Joppa [to get Peter]. About noon the next day, as they were on their journey and approaching the city, Peter went up on the roof to pray . . . . [S]uddenly the men sent by Cornelius appeared. They [said], 'Cornelius, a centurion, an upright and God-fearing man . . . was directed by a holy angel to send for you to come to his house and to hear what you have to say.' The next day [Peter] got up and went with them . . . . " (Acts 10:7–9, 17, 22, 23b)

JOURNEY

"We looked up the disciples [in Tyre] and stayed there for seven days. Through the Spirit they told Paul not to go on to Jerusalem. When our days there were ended, we left and proceeded on our journey; and all of them, with wives and children, escorted us outside the city. There we knelt down on the beach and prayed and said farewell to one another. Then we went on board the ship, and they returned home. When we had finished the voyage from Tyre, we arrived at Ptolemais; and we greeted the believers and stayed with them for one day. The next day we left and came to Caesarea . . . . [A] prophet named Agabus . . . came to us and took Paul's belt, bound his own feet and hands with it, and said, 'Thus says the Holy Spirit, "This is the way the Jews in Jerusalem will bind the man who owns this belt and will hand him over to the Gentiles."'" (Acts 21:4-8, 10-11)

Reflection: The author of Luke's Gospel is the same author who wrote the Acts of the Apostles to serve as volume 2 and to take the themes he associated with Jesus and apply them to the apostles, particularly Peter and Paul. Just as he presents Jesus on a journey as an example for Christians, so he presents Peter and Paul as examples of Christians on journeys who imitate Jesus. Keeping in mind that the first mission of the apostles after the resurrection was to the Jews, represented by Peter, the author of the Acts furthers that mission to the Gentiles, represented by Paul, but launched by Peter. He journeys to Caesarea and enters the home of the Gentile centurion Cornelius after having a vision and begins to preach about Jesus. Before he is finished, the Holy Spirit comes upon all who are gathered in Cornelius's home, and then all are baptized in the name of Jesus (Acts 10:24-48). After making his journey, Peter declares, "I truly understand that God shows no partiality" (Acts 10:34). Thus, the mission to the Gentiles is launched by Peter, but it is quickly picked up by Paul.

Paul makes many journeys in the Acts and narrates some in his letters (Rom 15:24; 2 Cor 11:26). The narrator character in the Acts of the Apostles, who suddenly appears at 16:10 and is never identified, tells about a stop in Tyre on one of Paul's journeys; Paul and his nameless travel companion stayed there with disciples for seven days before they board the ship and continued their journey to Caesarea, the same place previously visited by Peter. In two different places—Tyre and Caesarea—Paul is told not to travel to Jerusalem, but three days later they went anyway. Just as the Lukan Jesus' journey narrative ended in Jerusalem, so does the Lukan Paul's journey narrative end there. He is rejected by the Jews and, after two years in prison, he is handed over to the Gentiles, and taken to Rome. The Acts of the Apostles ends with Paul under house arrest in Rome and living there for two years (Acts 28:16–30).

Peter's and Paul's journeys are missionary; they are sent by God to bring the good news about Jesus' death and resurrection to the Gentiles—anyone who is not Jewish. The narrative structure of Luke-Acts is based on the journey motif; the goal is to get the gospel out of Jerusalem and to Rome. Today, the goal of the journey is to get the gospel out of our homes through the lives we modern day Gentiles live. Like Peter and Paul, we enter the chaos of our world. Peter entered a Gentile home, forbidden by the law. Paul proclaimed the very movement he had set out to destroy. Both were transformed by their journeys, just as we will be. According to tradition, Peter was crucified upside down, and Paul was beheaded with a sword. Their final transformation, after fulfilling their mission, was from death to eternal life in imitation of Jesus, who had died and been raised, as preached by Peter and Paul.

Meditation/Journal: In what specific ways do you bring your Christianity out of your home and into the world? What order do you leave behind? What chaos do you encounter? What reorder and transformation do you encounter?

Prayer: Father of Jesus, pour on me the gift of your Holy Spirit that I may be enlivened to bring the good news of your Son's death and resurrection to the world. With that same Spirit, guide my travels and put your words into my mouth. Give me the missionary courage of Peter and Paul to journey to you now and forever. Amen.

2

Road

Balaam on the Road

Scripture: " . . . Balaam got up in the morning, saddled his donkey, and went with the officials of Moab. God's anger was kindled because he was going, and the angel of the LORD took his stand in the road as his adversary. Now he was riding on the donkey . . . . The donkey saw the angel of the LORD standing in the road with a drawn sword in his hand; so the donkey turned off the road, and went into the field; and Balaam struck the donkey, to turn it back onto the road. Then the angel of the LORD stood in a narrow path between the vineyards, with a wall on either side. When the donkey saw the angel of the LORD, it scraped against the wall, and scraped Balaam's foot against the wall; so he struck it again. Then the angel of the LORD went ahead, and stood in a narrow place, where there was no way to turn either to the right or to the left. When the donkey saw the angel of the LORD, it lay down under Balaam; and Balaam's anger was kindled, and he struck the donkey with his staff. Then the LORD opened the mouth of the donkey, and it said to Balaam, 'What have I done to you that you have struck me these three times?' Then the LORD opened the eyes of Balaam, and he saw the angel of the LORD standing in the road . . . ; and he bowed down, falling on his face. The angel of the LORD said to Balaam, 'Go with the men; but speak only what I tell you to speak.' So Balaam went on with the officials of Balak." (Num 22:21–28, 31, 35)

Reflection: As the unique account of Balaam, his donkey, and the angel of the LORD makes clear, a journey is often made on a road, some kind of hard surfaced track upon which animals (donkeys, horses) with or without carts (wagons) can be ridden or led. However, a road can also be a way that leads toward some predictable outcome. Both meanings are operative here. Balak, king of Moab, feared the numerous Israelites (Num 22:1–6). In the hope of defeating the Israelites, he sends for the prophet Balaam, whom he wants to come and curse the Israelites; a biblical curse, composed of prophetic words in this case, invokes harm upon those cursed. Balak wants Balaam to send injury upon Israel, but God tells his prophet not to go with the messengers sent by Balak; the people Balak wants cursed are blessed by God (Num 22:12–13). So Balaam refuses to go (Num 22:14). Again, Balak sends messengers, and, again, Balaam refuses to go (Num 22:15–19). During the night, however, God tells Balaam to go, but he is to do only what God tells him. Seemingly, once Balaam sets out to meet Balak, God regrets his decision and places himself (referred to as "the angel of the LORD") in Balaam's way on the road three times, sparking Balaam's action of striking his beast of burden with his staff three times (Num 22:28). Finally, God reveals himself to Balaam by placing words in the donkey's mouth! Again, he is told to go with Balak's messengers, but he is to speak only what he is told. When he gets to Balak, he sees the camp of the Israelites. Instead of cursing them, to the astonishment of Balak (Num 23:11, 25; 24:10) he blesses them four times (Num 23:7–10, 18–24; 24:3–9, 15–24) before leaving Balak and taking the road home.

It is while he is journeying on the physical road that Balaam begins to understand that that road is the way to the predictable outcome that God intends, and that Balaam is the instrument for that outcome. The LORD, who has already blessed the Israelites by using Moses to get them out of Egypt to fulfill the promise he made to Abraham and his descendants, intends to bless them again before their enemy: Balak of Moab. The instrument is Balaam; the words are God's both in the donkey's mouth and in Balaam's mouth. This unique story features the LORD, who—biblically is in charge of the world he created—wants to be sure that Balaam will do what he is told and speak God's words of blessing over his chosen people. With careful reflection we discover that we have had experiences similar to those of Balaam. We decided what we were going to do, only to discover that it is not possible or we are hindered in some way from carrying it out. We decided what we were going to say to someone who hurt us in some way, only to accept his or her apology and cancel the words before they could emerge from our lips. Feeling something bothering us or thinking conscientiously about something is like Balaam's donkey squeezing us against the wall. If we find ourselves straying into a field or laid upon by a heavy load, we may have left the straight road of the journey and gone astray; like Balaam, a speechless donkey may speak with a human voice and restrain our prophetic madness (2 Pet 2:15–16).

Meditation/Journal: What journey on a physical road enabled you to understand that you were an instrument for the predictable outcome God intended? How did the LORD speak to you? What blessing did you deliver?

Prayer: Mighty God, you are not one who changes his mind. You have blessed your people, and you refuse to revoke it. Be with me on my journey, bless me, and put your words in my mouth. Grant that I may one day see you and praise you forever. Amen.

Lion on the Road

Scripture: "While Jeroboam was standing by the altar to offer incense, a man of God came out of Judah by the word of the LORD to Bethel and proclaimed against the altar by the word of the LORD. . . . Then the king said to the man of God, 'Come home with me and dine, and I will give you a gift.' But the man of God said to the king, . . . 'I was commanded by the word of the LORD: You shall not eat food, or drink water, or return by the way that you came.' Now there lived an old prophet in Bethel. [The old prophet] said to him, 'I also am a prophet as you are, and an angel spoke to me by the word of the LORD: Bring him back with you into your house so that he may eat food and drink water.' But he was deceiving him. Then the man of God went back with him, and ate food and drank water in his house. As they were sitting at the table, the word of the LORD came to the prophet . . . : 'Thus says the LORD: Because you have disobeyed the word of the LORD, and have not kept the commandment that the LORD your God commanded you, . . . your body shall not come to your ancestral tomb.' Then as he went away, a lion met him on the road and killed him. His body was thrown in the road, and the donkey stood beside it; the lion also stood beside the body. When the prophet who had brought him back from the way heard of it, he said, 'It is the man of God who disobeyed the word of the LORD; therefore the LORD has given him to the lion, which has torn him and killed him according to the word that the LORD spoke to him. . . .' [H]e went and found the body thrown in the road, with the donkey and the lion standing beside the body. The prophet took up the body of the man of God . . . and brought it back to the city, to mourn and to bury him. He laid the body in his own grave . . . . " (1 Kgs 13:1–2a, 7–8a, 9, 11a, 18–22, 24, 26, 28a, 29–30a)

Reflection: This biblical story about the man of God, the prophet, and the lion is not one most people have ever heard and few have ever read. It is set at the time of Jeroboam I of Israel (931–910 BCE), the king who formed a realm of the ten tribes of Israel in the north and succeeded from Judah after King Solomon died. He established the worship of the golden calf at Bethel (1 Kgs 12:29), where he is confronted by a nameless man of God sent on journey by the LORD from Judah. After speaking against the erection of the altar before the golden calf (idolatry), the man of God heals the king's hand when it withers in his attempt to seize the man of God (1 Kgs 13:4–6). Jeroboam invites the man of God to dine with him; the man of God explains that God has forbidden him from doing so because it would indicate approval of the shrine at Bethel (1 Kings 13:7–10). However, a nameless prophet in Bethel hears about the visit of the man of God, travels the road to find him, and deceives him by telling him that an angel told him to invite him to his home for food and drink; he accepts the invitation (1 Kgs 13:11–19), believing the prophet. While they are eating, the prophet receives the word of God that the man of God has disobeyed the LORD's instructions; his punishment is that he will not be buried in his ancestral tomb. On his way home, the man of God is met on the road and killed by a lion; the prophet hears about it, goes and gets the body, and buries the man of God in his own grave (1 Kgs 13:20–30). The motive for the prophet's deceit of the man of God is not given by the author. The message of the story is that the nameless man of God should have obeyed the LORD instead of trusting another nameless prophet. In other words, not only should he have abstained from food and drink, but he should have taken a different road home (1 Kgs 13:9, 17).

The nameless man of God hears the LORD's call to leave his home in the southern Kingdom of Judah and take the road to Bethel, near the border between Israel and Judah. He leaves the order of Judah to take a journey into the chaos of Israel. Faithfully, he delivers the word of the LORD he has heard, but, unfaithfully, he fails to obey the command not to eat and drink in Bethel; according to the author of the First Book of Kings, the only shrine approved by God is the Temple in Jerusalem in Judah. Because he disobeys God, he is plunged into more chaos instead of being transformed. A lion meets him on the road and kills him; he is not permitted burial in his ancestral tomb. In the Bible, it is customary for successive generations to be buried in the family tomb in Judah; the man of God's punishment is denial of this custom. He is buried in the prophet's tomb in Bethel. Instead of coming back to Judah transformed, the man of God rests in the tomb of the prophet in Bethel. It is easy to be deceived on the road; even a prophet can deliver an inaccurate message which adds to the chaos, removes the transformation, and leaves the traveler worse off than before he or she answered the call. If a lion is spotted, something is wrong.

Meditation/Journal: On what road have you answered the call to journey only to discover that you couldn't fulfill the terms? Explain how chaos kept you from transformation instead of aiding the process?

Prayer: Mighty God, open my ears to hear your call and strengthen my will to obey your commands. As I travel your roads, I place all my trust in you. May your Spirit help me discern your ways today, tomorrow, and forever. Amen.

Journey into God

Unknown Road

Scripture: "Thus says God, the LORD, who created the heavens and stretched them out, who spread out the earth and what comes from it, who gives breath to the people upon it and spirit to those who walk in it: . . . I have given you as a covenant to the people, a light to the nations, to open eyes that are blind . . . . I will lead the blind by a road they do not know, by paths they have not known I will guide them. I will turn the darkness before them into light, the rough places into level ground. These are the things I will do, and I will not forsake them." (Isa 42:5, 6c, 7a, 16)

Reflection: In the above passage from Second Isaiah, God calls and commissions a servant to do his bidding. Echoing the beginning of the book of Genesis, the LORD reminds the servant that he is the creator; he stretches out the heavens, like one pitches a tent on the firm earth. To the people on earth he gives the breath of life, and he instills spirit. The unnamed servant serves as a covenant, a solemn agreement between God and people. He gives the servant the specific instruction to be a light to the nations, that is, to all people. The Gentiles are blind to God, and their eyes will be opened. The Jews are in Babylonian captivity, and their eyes will be opened again to the LORD. The servant will be God's instrument for leading and guiding the blind on an unknown road and turning their darkness into light. In other words, the servant will be a new Moses, who led the Israelites out of Egyptian darkness, while "[t]he LORD went in front of them in a pillar of cloud by day, to lead them along the way, and in a pillar of fire by night, to give them light, so that they might travel by day and by night" (Exod 13:21). God does not abandon his people; just as he did once before, he chooses a servant to lead the blind home on an unknown road.

Biblically, God, who is in charge of the world he created and the people he placed on the earth, calls us to be his servants. He invites us to leave our secure, orderly lives and take the journey, whose objective is to be light for the blind on an unknown road of chaos. We often don't know the next stop to take on the path of life. What career do we choose? Do we take the job offer and move? Do we buy the house or rent? Do we have children sooner or later? At what age do we retire? We enter into the chaos of the questions on our lifetime journey, trusting God to lead us either directly or through another servant. We are not abandoned on our sacred journey. Yes, the road is not known; we have not been on it before, and, even if we had, we are blinded by the chaotic possibilities through which we travel. We've made this kind of trip before and arrived transformed. We can do it again and be transformed again on our spiritual journey.

Meditation/Journal: How have you experienced yourself being a servant of God? What order did you leave behind to answer the call to begin a journey through chaos? What was the journey? What transformation occurred before you arrived home?

Prayer: LORD God, creator of heaven and earth, giver of breath and spirit to people, reach out and take my hand and open my blind eyes, as I journey through life on this road that I do not know. Guide me on paths that lead through chaotic darkness to the enduring and transforming light of your presence. Amen.

Road Marker

Scripture: " . . . [T]hus says the LORD: . . . [M]y people have forgotten me . . .; they have stumbled in their ways, in the ancient roads, and have gone into bypaths, not the highway . . . . Set up road markers for yourself, make yourself guideposts; consider well the highway, the road by which you went." (Jer 18:13a, 15; 31:21a)

"The word of the LORD came to me [, Ezekiel,]: Mortal, mark out two roads for the sword of the king of Babylon to come; both of them shall issue from the same land. And make a signpost, make it for a fork in the road leading to a city; mark out the road for the sword to come to Rabbah of the Ammonites or to Judah and to Jerusalem the fortified. For the king of Babylon stands at the parting of the way, at the fork in the two roads, to use divination . . . . Into his right hand comes the lot for Jerusalem, to set battering rams, to call out for slaughter, for raising the battle cry, to set battering rams against the gates, to cast up ramps, to build siege towers. But to them it will seem like a false divination, . . . bringing about their capture." (Ezek 21:18–23)

Reflection: In the passage from Jeremiah, the HB (OT) prophet portrays God employing the road metaphor to explain the situation in which Jerusalem found herself in 587 BCE. Because the Israelites had forgotten their God, the LORD, they were like those stumbling on ancient roads; they had taken bypaths of idolatry. Instead of traveling the covenant highway, they were on the jeep roads of destruction. God exhorts them to get back on track by erecting road signs, guideposts, and stone cairns so they can find the highway and return to the LORD on the same road upon which they strayed. Because they didn't, Ezekiel records the LORD's words to him about making a signpost with two arrows, one pointing to Rabbah—Judah's ally—and one pointing to Jerusalem, Judah's capital. Ezekiel is told that Nebuchadnezzar, king of Babylon, will choose the fork in the road that leads to Jerusalem, which is well fortified, but which will fall to his sword in his right hand. He will lay siege to the city, and, once he captures it, destroy the Temple and the city walls and take every able-bodied man, woman, and child as captives of war to Babylon. According to the HB (OT) book of Lamentations, "The roads to Zion mourn, for no one comes to the festivals; all her gates are desolate . . . " (Lam 1:4).

Road markers or road signs show the way for the spiritual journey. Just like the numerous green highway signs indicating distance from one place to another or exits (forks in the road), the spiritual journey has road markers pointing the way to God. It is easy to get lost with so many possible roads to take to over-spending, over-eating, and over-indulging, while the spiritual road takes us to disciplined prayer, reflection, and Scripture. Those road markers, and others like them, are guideposts that keep us on track. In the mountains, cairns—piled stones used as markers—keep climbers and hikers on the trail; without them it is easy to wonder around, go astray, or get lost. The spiritual journey begins with hearing a call to leave some comfort and begin the journey into chaos that will transform us and leave us at the sign indicating the next road we need to take.

Meditation/Journal: During your lifetime journey, when have you discovered yourself to be on a bypath and not on the spiritual highway? What fork in the road did you take? What road markers steered you in the right direction?

Prayer: Save me, O LORD, by keeping my feet on the road to you. Let your Holy Spirit guide me throughout my journey that I may one day reach you transformed and singing your praise forever. Amen.

Road to Jerusalem

Scripture: "[Jesus, disciples, and the twelve] were on the road, going up to Jerusalem, and Jesus was walking ahead of them; they were amazed, and those who followed were afraid. He took the twelve aside again and began to tell them what was to happen to him, saying, 'See, we are going up to Jerusalem, and the Son of Man will be handed over to the chief priests and the scribes, and they will condemn him to death; then they will hand him over to the Gentiles; they will mock him, and spit upon him, and flog him, and kill him; and after three days he will rise again.'" (Mark 10:32–34)

Reflection: The passage above marks what is known as the third passion prediction in Mark's Gospel. A passion prediction features the Markan Jesus telling his followers what is going to happen to him. It is a literary device employed by the author of a story and designed to keep the reader reading to see if the predicted event takes place. The omniscient author knows that the event will take place, because he is writing the story and knows how he wants it to end. In other words, this is the summary of Mark 14:1—16:8a. Thus, the author of Mark's Gospel presents Jesus leading a procession of people journeying on the road up to Jerusalem located in the mountains; in Mark's Gospel, this is the only trip to Jerusalem that Jesus takes. There are two responses presented; the disciples are amazed, but the twelve are afraid. Amazement is a response often given by observant disciples in Mark (2:12; 5:20; 12:17; 15:5). Fear characterizes the twelve in Mark (4:40; 6:50; 9:32) and some others (Mark 5:15; 11:18, 32; 16:8); once Jesus is arrested, they desert him and flee (Mark 14:50, 52, 72b). The Markan Jesus addresses his remarks on the road to the twelve, who fail to understand for the third time and make an inappropriate response (Mark 8:31–33; 9:30–34; 10:35–45). Mark's Gospel ends with all of the twelve men having run away, Jesus dying on the cross alone while a group of women observe from a distance, and the introduction of a new character—Joseph of Arimathea—who takes Jesus' body and places it in a tomb (Mark 15:40–47). Three days later, three of the observant women go to the tomb to anoint Jesus' body, find the tomb empty, and flee in terror and amazement (Mark 16:1–8a). Thus, all that Jesus had predicted on the road to Jerusalem had taken place!

We may not be on the road to Jerusalem, but we are always on the road to somewhere. And like the omniscient storyteller who wrote Mark's Gospel, when we tell a tale about an experience, we predict what will happen to us, because we have lived it already. We begin a sentence by saying, "I didn't know it then, but . . . . " Sometimes we even get ahead of ourselves in the linear progression of our story, have to back up chronologically, and get caught up with ourselves again. Narrating an experience with ourselves at the head is like a procession on the road to Jerusalem. As the elements in our tale unfold, we employ words to move forward our listeners. Some will be amazed, expressing sentiments of good luck, divine protection, or salvation by God. Others will express how fearful they would have been, because fear paralyzes many people as they journey on the road to Jerusalem—or elsewhere!

Meditation/Journal: What has been a recent experience on the road to Jerusalem? To whom did you narrate it? How did you employ prediction in your narrative? Which listeners were amazed? Which listeners were afraid?

Prayer: I thank you, Father, Lord of heaven and earth, for the example of Jesus' journey to Jerusalem. Help me to follow him through suffering and death to the life of resurrection, where he lives and reigns with you and the Holy Spirit, one God, forever and ever. Amen.

Road from Jerusalem

Scripture: " . . . [A]n angel of the Lord said to Philip, 'Get up and go toward the south to the road that goes down from Jerusalem to Gaza.' (This is a wilderness road.) So he got up and went. Now there was an Ethiopian eunuch, a court official of the Candace, queen of the Ethiopians, in charge of her entire treasury. He had come to Jerusalem to worship and was returning home; seated in his chariot, he was reading the prophet Isaiah. Then the Spirit said to Philip, 'Go over to this chariot and join it.' So Philip ran up to it and heard him reading the prophet Isaiah." (Acts 8:26–30a)

Reflection: In the last reflection, we went up to Jerusalem; in this reflection, we come down from Jerusalem. The story about the Ethiopian eunuch is narrated by the author of the Acts of the Apostles—the second volume to Luke's Gospel—to demonstrate how the gospel traveled from Jerusalem to Ethiopia, south of Egypt in Africa. The agent is God in the person of an angel; the minister is Philip, who has been instructed to take the wilderness road from Jerusalem that passes through Gaza. The recipient of ministry is the Ethiopian eunuch, who was placed in a position of trust—treasurer—of the queen of Ethiopia. It was not uncommon for non-Jews (Gentiles) to come to Jerusalem to worship Israel's LORD. While he was sitting in his chariot, which was being driven by someone else, he was reading aloud from the fourth suffering servant poem on a scroll of the prophet Isaiah (53:7–8). Not only is God, under the appearance of an angel of the Lord, directing Philip to take the wilderness road, but God, under the name of the Spirit, is directing the meeting of Philip and the Ethiopian eunuch, who is reading about the suffering servant who, "like a lamb that is led to the slaughter, and like a sheep that before its shearers is silent, so he did not open his mouth" (Isa 53:7). Philip uses the occasion to catechize the eunuch by telling him that the passage accurately describes the suffering and death of Jesus, but the good news is that God raised him from the dead. Under the direct guidance of God, Philip performs a hermeneutic on the Isaian passage revealing the suffering servant of God to have been Jesus. When they come to some water along the road, they stop the chariot, and both get out. Philip baptizes the eunuch, and then "the Spirit of the Lord snatche[s] Philip away" (Acts 8:39). In other words, God has accomplished what he set out to do along the road and now moves Philip to a new location (Acts 8:40). One never knows what can happen on the wilderness road from Jerusalem to Ethiopia!

While chariot travel is a means of transportation of the past, road travel is very much a thing of the present. A road trip, indicating that it takes place in a car or a hybrid of such, may have God behind it. Getting lost on a back road in Kansas, Colorado, or Montana may—or may not—have a divine agent directing the hands steering the wheel of the vehicle. For some reason, an angel of the Lord baptizes us into the beauty of a wheat field swaying in the wind or corn field with beige tassels reaching for the heavens. Seeing the beauty of a chain of mountains pocked with snowfields can take away one's breath. And there is nothing that teaches the meaning of distance and reminds us of how small we are than big sky country. The back-road diversion may end with the chance meeting of someone interesting at a gas station, a restaurant, or a motel. We may discover ourselves voicing a psalm of praise simply by speaking about the grace surrounding us on the wilderness road.

Meditation/Journal: When have you taken a road less traveled? Who was the agent? Who was the minister? What new experiences were opened out to you on the road?

Prayer: I praise you, LORD, for wilderness roads, for guiding angels, for ministers who do your will. I praise you, LORD, for sun and moon, for fields of grain, for mountains, and for heavens that never touch the earth. I praise and exalt your name, O LORD, today, tomorrow, and forever. Amen.

Know the Road

Scripture: Tobias said to his father Tobit, " . . . I do not know the roads to Media, or how to get there." Raphael said to Tobias, " . . . I am acquainted with [Media] and know all the roads." Raphael said to Tobit, "I can go with [Tobias] and I know all the roads, for I have often gone to Media and have crossed all its plains, and I am familiar with its mountains and all of its roads." After Tobias and Raphael went on their journey, Tobit's wife, Anna, "would rush out every day and watch the road her son had taken . . . . Anna sat looking intently down the road by which her son would come." (Tob 5:2c, 6a, 10l; 10:7d; 11:5)

Reflection: The OT (A) book of Tobit, a novella, features a journey taken by Tobias and Raphael from Nineveh to Media and back. After Tobias searches for someone who knows the road to accompany him from Nineveh to Media, he finds Raphael, although he does not recognize him as God in the person of an angel. Raphael, who knows the roads, agrees to guide Tobias to Media to retrieve some money Tobit left in deposit there. While they are gone for a long time on their adventure, Tobit's wife, Anna, who is presented as a worrier, often leaves their home every day and watches the road the travelers had taken in the hope of discovering them returning on the same road. Thus, in the story it is important to know the road, to watch the road, and to trust the guide. Since GPS had not yet been invented, Tobit, Anna, and Tobias rely upon Raphael to know the way.

With an angel present in the story, it is not difficult to conclude that this is a spiritual journey in addition to it being a physical one. As a spiritual journey, we must know the road to the Spirit; that road is paved with prayer, Scripture, reflection, and meditation. Watching the road involves growth in prayer, in biblical reading and understanding, in application to our lives and to the world in which we live today. Often, we need a guide, who is sometimes called a spiritual director. This is a person who is some type of spiritual master, one we can trust, that is, one who has the experience of knowing the road and having watched it for a long time. He or she is able to suggest further ways for us to know and watch the road which brings growth and development into our lives. A spiritual director may be an angel in disguise, an instrument of God, who desires that we never stop traveling into him. The journey ends only when we have finished taking our last breath. Then, the road we have known and watched leads us to the same God who has called us to take the journey.

Meditation/Journal: How well do you know your spiritual road? How much time daily do you spend watching it? Who has served as your guide along the way?

Prayer: "You are righteous, O Lord, and all your deeds are just; all your ways are mercy and truth; you judge the world. And now, O Lord, remember me and look favorably upon me" (Tob 3:2–3a). Send your angel to guide me safely on the road to you. Amen.

Thorns on the Road

Scripture: "Just as in an olive orchard three or four olives may be left on every tree, or just as, when a vineyard is gathered, some clusters may be left by those who search carefully through the vineyard, so in those days three or four shall be left by those who search their houses with the sword. The earth shall be left desolate, and its fields shall be plowed up, and its roads and all its paths shall bring forth thorns, because no sheep will go along them." (2 Esd 16:29–32)

Reflection: The material in chapters 15 and 16 of the OT (A) book of Second Esdras is motivated by the author's belief that the end of the world is at hand. The passage above first describes the devastation of humankind from famine, and those who survive the famine will die by the sword (2 Esd 16:18–28). Only a fraction of humankind will be spared; it will be like three or four olives left on a tree that has been firmly shaken, or like three or four clusters of grapes in a vineyard carefully searched that have been hidden by grape leaves. The images are also found in the prophet Isaiah, who writes about the glory of Jacob being brought low: " . . . [I]t shall be as when reapers gather standing grain and their arms harvest the ears . . . . Gleanings will be left in [the field], as when an olive tree is beaten—two or three berries in the top of the highest bough, four or five on the branches of a fruit tree, says the LORD God of Israel" (Isa 17:5–6). Second, the author describes the desolation of the earth; the fields will be plowed over, and the no-longer-used roads and paths will sprout thorns. The song of the vineyard (Isa 5:1–7) contains the same destructive note as that found in Second Esdras. It is presented as a vineyard metaphor for Israel and Judah; because the vineyard yields only wild grapes, the owner states that he " . . . will make it a waste; it shall not be pruned or hoed, and it shall be overgrown with briers and thorns" (Isa 5:6a). In the CB (NT), Jesus' parable about the sower and the seed features some seed that fell among thorns, "and the thorns grew up and choked it, and it yielded no grain" (Mark 4:7; cf. Matt 13:7, Luke 8:7).

While such apocalyptic discourse continues to permeate the culture in books, films, and internet, the big bang doesn't seem to be in any hurry to reverse itself anytime soon! Furthermore, the destruction of creation contradicts the proclamation of its goodness by the author of the first account of creation (Gen 1:4, 10b, 12b, 18b, 21b, 25b, 31). Apocalyptic writers—both ancient and modern—do not usually think through the logic of their pronouncements. No one disagrees that there are thorns on the road, as Second Esdras states, or that thorns choke the seed that falls where they grow, as Jesus states. Thorns on the roads and paths continue to disrupt the spiritual journey. One such thorn is consumerism; a person can so identify himself or herself with what he or she buys that the care of stuff can leave little or no time to keep traveling. Another thorn is individualism; being the only person who matters negates the wisdom of others on the spiritual quest. Relativism is a thorn that dictates that meaning is assigned by the individual with no recourse to the common good of the community. There is nothing wrong with owning property, a home, or a car, as long as we are detached from such things, realizing that both they and we are passing away.

Meditation/Journal: What thorns have you encountered on your lifetime journey into God? What did the thorns choke in you? What chaos did you pass through to be transformed?

Prayer: Holy One, protect me from destruction. With your Mighty Spirit guide my feet to roads and paths free from thorns. May the words of your Son, Jesus Christ, produce abundant grace in me during my journey into you. You are one God—Father, Son, and Holy Spirit—forever. Amen.

ROAD

Easy Road/Hard Road

Scripture: Jesus said to his disciples: "Enter through the narrow gate; for the gate is wide and the road is easy that leads to destruction, and there are many who take it. For the gate is narrow and the road is hard that leads to life, and there are few who find it." (Matt 7:13–14)

Reflection: Near the end of the first discourse Jesus gives in Matthew's Gospel, he warns his disciples against complacency and misplaced security. Traveling the easy road does not take a person through transformation; rather, it leads to destruction for those who travel that way. The author of the OT (A) book of Sirach presents the same wisdom: "Do not be overconfident on a smooth road, and give good heed to your paths" (Sir 32:21–22). The road to a lifetime of transformation is hard; that is why few find it. While we should not "go on a path full of hazards" (Sir 32:20), we should pay attention to the OT (A) prophet Baruch's words to exiled Jews: "My children, endure with patience the wrath that has come upon you from God. My pampered children have traveled rough roads" (Bar 4:25a, 26a). The rough roads the exiles have traveled—both literally and figuratively—will strengthen them to hear God's call to return to Jerusalem. Those who chose to leave Babylon and returned discovered how hard that road was; that is why only a few did it.

Taking the path of least resistance leaves us unchanged; such a status, according to the Matthean Jesus, leads to self-destruction. We bask in the ordered lives we live. We have ears, but we cannot hear; we live our lives with our fingers stuck in our ears. If we hear the call to leave order and enter into chaos, we may have to act on what we have heard and prepare for and take the life-giving journey that transforms us. The spiritual journey that leads to life constantly points us to answer the divine call to prepare for the trip and leave security behind. Freely, we enter the chaos of the journey, knowing that getting back home will reveal the destruction of our once-protective city walls and our prized Temple. However, unless we take the journey into chaos, we cannot see how our misplaced security prohibits our being transformed into deeper life.

Meditation/Journal: When have you taken the easy road? What were the consequences for your spiritual journey? When have you taken the hard road? What were the consequences for your spiritual journey?

Prayer: LORD God, send your Holy Spirit to guide my deliberations when I hear you call me to travel further toward you. Guide my footsteps on the hard road traveled by Jesus, your Son, through the narrow gate to eternal life with you forever. Amen.

Roadside

Scripture: "As [Jesus] and his disciples and a large crowd were leaving Jericho, Bartimaeus son of Timaeus, a blind beggar, was sitting by the roadside. When he heard that it was Jesus of Nazareth, he began to shout out and say, 'Jesus, Son of David, have mercy on me!' Many sternly ordered him to be quiet, but he cried out even more loudly, 'Son of David, have mercy on me!' Jesus stood still and said, 'Call him here.' And they called the blind man, saying to him, 'Take heart; get up, he is calling you.' So throwing off his cloak, he sprang up and came to Jesus. Then Jesus said to him, 'What do you want me to do for you?' The blind man said to him, 'My teacher, let me see again.' Jesus said to him, 'Go, your faith has made you well.' Immediately he regained his sight and followed him on the way." (Mark 10:46b–52)

Reflection: Sometimes it is on the side of the road where one is transformed. This narrative has been edited by the author of Matthew's Gospel to display his penchant for doubles; in this case Mark's single, named, blind man roadside becomes Matthew's double, unnamed, blind men roadside (Matt 20:29–34). Luke edits the account by expanding it and presenting a single, unnamed, blind man roadside (Luke 18:35–43); however, this author presents the roadside blind man declaring Jesus to be the son of David two times, just like Matthew presents his two blind men doing. The Markan author features the roadside blind man twice declaring Jesus to be son of David. In Luke's version, Jesus fulfills his anointed mission to give sight to the blind (Luke 4:18; cf. Isa 61:1; 35:5). Behind all three accounts of the roadside encounter are the words of Deuteronomy: "Cursed be anyone who misleads a blind person on the road" (Deut 27:18a). Also, all three accounts presume that the roadside blind man or men were not always blind; at one time they could see.

In other words, at one point in their lives the blind possessed the order of seeing, but blindness plunged them into chaos. All they can do is sit by the side of the road and inquire from passersby who might be near them. Thus, they hear the call from members of the crowd: Jesus of Nazareth is passing by. That call enables them to shout again to get the son of David's attention. After doing so, they tell him that they want to see. They want to be healed physically, but they also want to see spiritually. This latter fact is more significant in Mark's Gospel; the blind man sees what Jesus' disciples do not! Once Jesus gives back their sight, they, now transformed, follow him. They resume the journey they were on before they became blind. Bartimaeus follows Jesus on the way, on the road, on the journey. Matthew's two blind men do the same. Luke's unnamed blind man follows Jesus while glorifying God; those who witnesses this, according to Luke, praised God for what they had seen roadside.

Meditation/Journal: What experience of your life has left you blind? What call did you hear and answer? What journey did you take? How was your blindness transformed into sight?

Prayer: I praise you, LORD! I sing a new song to you! Out of my darkness you have brought light. Guide me on the way, deliver me from all blindness, and lead me to the eternal brightness that will transform me into you forever. Amen.

Cloaks on the Road

Scripture: "[Two of Jesus' disciples] brought the colt to Jesus and threw their cloaks on it; and he sat on it. Many people spread their cloaks on the road, and others spread leafy branches that they had cut in the fields." (Mark 11:7–8)

Reflection: On what is referred to as Palm Sunday—the Sunday preceding Easter Sunday—the passage from Mark's Gospel is translated into the action of people holding, and maybe processing with, palm branches. Only John's Gospel declares that the crowd "took branches of palm trees and went out to meet [Jesus]" (John 12:12). A careful reading of Mark's account above reveals that unspecified leafy branches were cut in the fields. The author of Matthew's Gospel transforms the Markan account into a donkey and colt, upon whom the disciples place their cloaks for Jesus to sit. "A very large crowd spread their cloaks on the road, and others cut branches from the trees and spread them on the road," according to Matthew (21:8). The Lukan account of this event features two of Jesus' disciples fetching a colt, throwing their cloaks on it, and seating Jesus on top of the colt and the cloaks (Luke 19:35). "As he rode along, people kept spreading their cloaks on the road," records Luke (19:36). There is no mention at all of leafy branches! So, based upon the evidence, the Sunday before Easter Sunday should be named Cloak Sunday, since cloaks on both the donkey and/or colt and on the road are what is common to the synoptic gospels of Mark, Matthew, and Luke!

Jesus is on the road to Jerusalem. The cloaks spread on the road indicate that Jesus is being welcomed by the crowd as royalty. In the ancient world, when a king or emperor came to town, he was greeted by his subjects' act of submission and homage, namely, placing their outer cloaks on the surface of the road over which the ruler rode or walked. In the same way one would spread covers on a bed, the people spread cloaks on the road to welcome Jesus. This was a political demonstration or a modern massive march. Underlying the cloak-spreading action are the words of the HB (OT) prophet Zechariah: "Rejoice greatly, O daughter Zion! Shout aloud, O daughter Jerusalem! Lo, your king comes to you; triumphant and victorious is he, humble and riding on a donkey, on a colt, the foal of a donkey" (Zech 9:9). According to the crowd, Jesus is the new king reviving the Davidic dynasty (Mark 11:9–10; Matt 21:9; Luke 19:38). This was a way of speaking against imperial power while greeting divine power. In other words, by spreading their cloaks on the road, the crowd who went ahead of Jesus into Jerusalem and those who followed behind were making a statement that was read loudly and clearly by those representing imperial power and watching the road!

Meditation/Journal: As you journey, what kind of statement (march, demonstration, yard sign, etc.) have you made about governmental power? How was that statement equivalent to the crowds at the time of Jesus spreading their cloaks on the road?

Prayer: Hosanna! Blessed is the one who comes in your name, O LORD! He, the Son of David, is the king, who brings peace to earth and glory to you in heaven. Grant me a share in the kingdom of him who lives and reigns forever and forever. Amen.

ROAD

Talking on the Road

Scripture: "... [T]wo of [Jesus' disciples] were going to a village called Emmaus, about seven miles from Jerusalem, and talking with each other about all [the] things that had happened. While they were talking and discussing, Jesus himself came near and went with them, but their eyes were kept from recognizing him.... [H]e said to them, 'Oh, how foolish you are, and how slow of heart to believe all that the prophets have declared! Was it not necessary that the Messiah should suffer these things and then enter into his glory?' When he was at the table with them, he took bread, blessed and broke it, and gave it to them. Then their eyes were opened, and they recognized him; and he vanished from their sight. They said to each other, 'Were not our hearts burning within us while he was talking to us on the road, while he was opening the scriptures to us?'" (Luke 24:13–16, 25–26, 30–32)

Reflection: In the passage above from Luke's Gospel, there are two conversations taking place. The first is between the two disciples on the road from Jerusalem to Emmaus. They are talking about the things that had taken place in the past few days: Jesus of Nazareth's crucifixion, death, and resurrection. It is while they are talking and discussing those things that Jesus appears, walks with them, and joins in the second conversation with them. They don't recognize him, as he asks them about what they are talking and discussing as they walk on to Emmaus. He contributes to the conversation by reminding them that it was necessary, according to the prophets, that the Messiah should suffer, die, and be raised to glory. Once they reach Emmaus, he agrees to spend the night with them by first eating dinner. After the three are seated at the table, he takes bread, blesses it, breaks it, and gives it to them. With that action, they recognize who had joined in their conversation on the road, but he has vanished before they can say more. Then, reflecting upon their talking and discussing on the road with Jesus, they remember that their hearts were burning within them while he was talking with them and opening scriptures to them. One never knows who the stranger on the road may be as talking and discussing ensue.

We live in a culture that has taught us to distrust the stranger on the road and not engage in conversation with him or her. While one should, nevertheless, be cautious, the unique Lukan story advises us not to reach absolute decisions about conversations with strangers on the road. If the COVID-19 pandemic did nothing else, it fostered neighbors talking to each other while walking on city streets with or without their dogs. People who lived next door to each other for years left their quarantined homes for a walk and met each other and talked to each other. Some didn't even know the names of their neighbors, but through the simplest of conversations—about the weather, politics, economy, etc.—they learned each other's names and the names of their dogs and talked to each other. Some were surprised by what they heard; some had no idea how interesting that person in the neighborhood could be. Others exchanged tips about yards or flower seeds or trees. They discovered doctors, nurses, veterinarians, small business owners, etc. living all around them. And upon more talking concluded that they didn't know who the stranger on the road was as the talking and discussing ensued.

Meditation/Journal: What have you discovered about the stranger on the road while talking and discussing with him or her? What have you discovered about yourself on your journey while talking and discussing with the stranger on the road?

Prayer: Son of God, you teach me that where two or three are gathered together, you are there in my midst. Make my heart burn within me as I encounter you through walking, talking, and discussing with the stranger on the road. Jesus, you are Lord forever and ever. Amen.

Fig Tree Beside the Road

Scripture: "In the morning, when [Jesus left Bethany], . . . he returned to the city [of Jerusalem]; he was hungry. And seeing a fig tree by the side of the road, he went to it and found nothing at all on it but leaves. Then he said to it, 'May no fruit ever come from you again!' And the fig tree withered at once. When the disciples saw it, they were amazed, saying, 'How did the fig tree wither at once?' Jesus answered them, 'Truly I tell you, if you have faith and do not doubt, not only will you do what has been done to the fig tree, but even if you say to this mountain, "Be lifted up and thrown into the sea," it will be done. Whatever you ask for in prayer with faith, you will receive.'" (Matt 21:18–22)

Reflection: The origin of the fig-tree-beside-the-road story found in Matthew's Gospel is a two-stage account found in Mark's Gospel (11:12–14, 20–24). In Mark's narrative, the cursing of the fig tree and its demise frames the cleansing of the Temple in Jerusalem (Mark 11:15–19), a technique—called intercalating[1]—employed elsewhere in this author's work (Mark 5:21–43; 6:6b–32; and others). Even though the author states "it was not the season for figs" (Mark 11:13b), the lack of fruitfulness represents the city's and Temple's inability to do God's will and may even reflect the destruction of both in 70 CE by the Romans. Not only has Matthew removed the two-stage development he found in Mark, but he has removed the note about it not being the season for figs and turned the account into an immediate miracle story. In Mark, a day passes before Jesus and his disciples see "the fig tree withered away to its roots" (Mark 11:20). Also, Peter gets a line to speak about "the fig tree that [Jesus] cursed [the day before; it] has withered" (Mark 11:21b), which Matthew has removed and turned into a question about how did the fig tree wither at once (Matt 21:20). Both the discovery of the withered fig tree in Mark and the immediate withering of it in Matthew provide the occasion for Jesus to teach about the power of words spoken out of faith. With faith in God—and without doubt— disciples are able to command a mountain to be lifted up and thrown into the sea (Mark 11:23; Matt 21:21). In fact, whatever disciples ask in prayer, if they believe that they have received it, it will be theirs (Mark 11:24; Matt 21:22). The reader has to keep in mind that this was sparked by a fig tree beside the road!

At the time of Jesus, a fig tree beside the road represented peace and prosperity. But the fig tree was barren of fruit, indicating that Jesus' world was barren of peace and prosperity. The phrase *peace and prosperity* means that people are doing well financially because they are not at war, but at the time of Matthew's writing, around 80 CE, the Jews had been at war with the Romans and lost. Jesus' act of cursing the fig tree, which was already barren, further indicates that peace and prosperity did not exist. Modern fig trees, signs of peace and prosperity, include a three-bedroom home with a two-car garage, a six-digit bank account balance protected by the FDIC, a country without domestic troubles, and a world without international conflicts. If Jesus walked our roads or city streets today, where might he be drawn to satisfy his hunger? McDonalds? Taco Bell? Arby's? There are a lot of fig trees by the side of the road, and it is only with faithful prayer that they can be controlled.

---

1. One story is begun only to be interrupted by a second story; after the conclusion of the second story, the first story is resumed and completed.

Meditation/Journal: What are the fig trees beside your spiritual journey road? Do they provide you with food? What have you asked for in prayer with faith that you received?

Prayer: Father, you have made the world your house of prayer for all people. As I make my journey into you, deepen my faith in you and bring forth good deeds from me for all I meet beside the road. You are God forever and ever. Amen.

Crossroads

Scripture: "Does not wisdom call, and does not understanding raise her voice? On the heights, beside the way, at the crossroads she takes her stand; beside the gates in front of the town, at the entrance of the portals she cries out: 'To you, O people, I call, and my cry is to all that live. O simple ones, learn prudence; acquire intelligence, you who lack it.'" (Prov 8:1–5)

Reflection: A crossroads is an intersection, a place where two or more roads meet or cross each other. At the crossroads is where we find Woman Wisdom. In the HB (OT) book of Proverbs, wisdom is personified as a woman, who yells from the mountains, beside the roads, at the crossroads, and before the city gates an invitation to learn prudence—good sense—and to acquire intelligence—the ability to think and learn! She declares that God created her at the beginning of his creation, then she served him like a master worker delighting in humankind (Prov 8:22–31). She desires that people listen to her instruction, becoming wise, and keep her ways (Prov 8:32–34). Woman Wisdom is the master teacher, who instructs the human race and brings about understanding for those on a spiritual journey. She states, " . . . [W]hoever finds me finds life and obtains favor from the LORD" (Prov 8:35). The HB (OT) prophet Jeremiah records similar words from God: "Thus says the LORD: Stand at the crossroads, and look, and ask for the ancient paths, where the good way lies; and walk in it, and find rest for your souls" (Jer 6:16a).

On our lifetime journey, we come to many crossroads, where we have the opportunity to learn prudence and to acquire intelligence. Common sense, sound practical judgement derived from experience, teaches us that our lifetime journey involves hearing the LORD's call to leave order behind, prepare for and take the trip, knowing that the result will be transformation.

The prudence crossroads is the accumulation of all the living we have done and reflected upon deeply. It may also include the experiences others have shared with us. Learning from experience is an art form! From study—in high school, college, reading, internet, podcasts, etc.—we acquire the ability to engage in critical thinking, disciplined intellectual criticism that combines research, knowledge of historical context, and balanced judgment to exercise intelligence. All those skills, coupled with understanding of Scripture, bring us to the crossroads, where we seek to travel the ancient paths, where the good way lies.

Meditation/Journal: While on your spiritual journey, to what crossroads did you come? What prudence did you learn? What intelligence did you acquire?

Prayer: At the beginning of your work, O LORD, you created wisdom to be your master worker. Help me to learn prudence and to acquire intelligence from your Holy Spirit that at the crossroads of my spiritual journey I may find life and obtain your favor now and forever. Amen.

Streets, Lanes, and Roads

Scripture: Jesus said: "Someone gave a great dinner and invited many. At the time for the dinner he sent his slave to say to those who had been invited, 'Come; for everything is ready now.' But they all alike began to make excuses. So the slave returned and reported this to his master. Then the owner of the house became angry and said to his slave, 'Go out at once into the streets and lanes of the town and bring in the poor, the crippled, the blind, and the lame.' And the slave said, 'Sir, what you ordered has been done, and there is still room.' Then the master said to the slave, 'Go out into the roads and lanes, and compel people to come in, so that my house may be filled.'" (Luke 14:16–18a, 21–23)

Reflection: On the surface, Luke's version of the parable of the great dinner, as told by Jesus while dining with a leader of the Pharisees, seems to be a story about the regrets of those who had been invited originally to share a great dinner. But under the surface, Jesus' parable of the kingdom violates the Torah regulation that "no one who has a blemish shall draw near, one who is blind or lame, or one who has a mutilated face or a limb too long, or one who has a broken foot or a broken hand, or a hunchback, or a dwarf, or a man with a blemish in his eyes or an itching disease or scabs or crushed testicles" (Lev 21:18–20). In other words, the person giving the dinner party is not concerned about contacting impurity or uncleanness from those who had been so designated by the Law. The host directs his servant to go out onto the streets, lanes, and roads and invite and compel those who were unclean to come to the feast. As soon as the impure enter his house, he will become impure and unclean! According to the parable, all are included; no one is an outcast.

As we make our spiritual journey, the parable reminds us not to separate people in any way. What excluded anyone with a blemish in the past no longer keeps him or her away in Jesus' world. Not only are the impure and unclean invited, they are compelled to attend! From the streets, lanes, and roads we, too, are invited and compelled to join enemies, murderers, rapists, child abusers, etc. at the feast. We come to the soup kitchen or shelter with the poor, the crippled, the blind, and the lame. To separate ourselves from others, according to the parable, means that "none of those who were invited will taste [the] dinner" (Luke 14:24). As he does elsewhere, the Lukan Jesus reduces all people to one common denominator: All are invited to the dinner. Those from the streets, lanes, and roads will feast in the kingdom of God (Luke 14:15).

Meditation/Journal: Along your spiritual journey, where have you found yourself separated from others, considered to be the poor, the crippled, the blind, and the lame from the streets, lanes, and roads? Along your spiritual journey, where have you found yourself included with the poor, the crippled, the blind and the lame from the streets, lanes, and roads?

Prayer: Father, in your kingdom you declare blessed those whom the world considers to be poor, crippled, blind, and lame. Keep me safe on the streets, lanes, and roads that lead to you that I may come with all to share dinner with you forever. Amen.

3

Path

Path of the LORD

Scripture: "Many peoples shall come and say, 'Come, let us go up to the mountain of the LORD, to the house of the God of Jacob; that he may teach us his ways and that we may walk in his paths.' For out of Zion shall go forth instruction, and the word of the LORD from Jerusalem." (Isa 2:3)

Reflection: The passage above from the HB (OT) prophet Isaiah is also found in the HB (OT) prophet Micah (4:2). Both pericopes echo Moses' words to the Israelites in the HB (OT) book of Deuteronomy: "You must follow exactly the path that the LORD your God has commanded you, so that you may live, and that it may go well with you, that you may live long in the land that you are to possess" (Deut 5:33). The passages refer both to a physical path and a metaphorical path. The physical path is a track that is made by people using it continuously, such as found frequently on college campuses. It may be paved, made for walking and/or cycling. Metaphorically, it refers to a course of action or a way of living according to the LORD's instruction emanating from Jerusalem. In the book of Deuteronomy, it serves as a double entendre, referring to both at the same time. The Israelites, who have been on a path to the promised land are getting ready to cross the Jordan River; then, they will have more physical paths to follow along with the spiritual paths from God that will provide them with a long life.

Job states that God watches all his paths, even setting a boundary to the soles of his feet (Job 13:27; cf. 33:11). Because the LORD loves people and desires their good, he opens before them a physical track upon which to tread. Also, he gives guidelines for how to live while one journeys over the path. In the HB (OT), those guidelines consist of three-hundred sixty-five precepts (many people have heard of ten of them), known as the Law or Torah. In the CB (NT), Jesus reduces those to two commandments: love God and love the neighbor as one loves one's self. In one of his loftier visions, the prophet Isaiah sees many nations streaming to the Temple on Mount Zion in Jerusalem to be catechized in the LORD's instructions about walking in his paths. According to Isaiah, the word of God about traveling in the path of the LORD is like a bull horn echoing from Jerusalem. For those who choose God's path, the Holy One's way offers long life and safe travels.

Meditation/Journal: What ways of the LORD do you follow while walking his path? What travel instructions have you received? Have long life and safe travels been yours? Explain.

Prayer: LORD, I follow your path to your mountain and your house that I may learn your ways. With your word, instruct me and guide the soles of my feet into a long life under your watchful care. Lead me in the path that takes me to the eternal Jerusalem, where I will live with you forever. Amen.

PATH

Paths of the Seas

Scripture: "I am the LORD, your Holy One, the Creator of Israel, your King. Thus says the LORD, who makes a way in the sea, a path in the mighty waters, who brings out chariot and horse, army and warrior; they lie down, they cannot rise, they are extinguished, quenched like a wick: I am about to do a new thing . . . . " (Isa 43:15–17, 19a)

Reflection: To write about a path through the sea is to engage in metaphor, a comparison of a path on land to reference Moses' action of lifting up his staff and stretching out his hand over the sea to divide it so that the Israelites could cross on dry ground (Exod 14:16). Psalm 77 references the exodus event, stating, "Your way [, O God,] was through the sea, your path, through the mighty waters; yet your footprints were unseen" (Ps 77:19). Psalm 8 employs the same metaphor to describe how God has given human beings dominion over "whatever passes along the paths of the seas" (Ps 8:8). The OT (A) book of Wisdom reflects upon the artistic wisdom of those who build a ship, then the author declares, " . . . [I]t is your providence, O Father, that steers its course, because you have given it a path in the sea, and a safe way through the waves" (Wis 14:3). Today, we would write about the wake, the track in the water left by a vessel or any other body moving through it. We might also compare it to the migration routes followed by many different creatures with whom we share the earth. The game trails in the mountains and forests are tracks to water and food. All of those are like paths in the seas, a route followed by many.

The Israelites considered their exodus through the Sea of Reeds to be the major salvation event of their spiritual journey out of Egyptian slavery to the freedom of the promised land. After walking the path through the sea, the providence of the LORD their God steered them to the country he had promised to Abraham, Isaac, and Jacob. The Israelites were migrants, following a route established and led by the God who left no footprints. The LORD, who had created a path in the Sea of Reeds, promised through the prophet Isaiah to do something new. He would again lead his people out of the slavery of Babylon to the land of Israel. The Jews would repeat the journey of their ancestors; they would leave the chaos behind, follow the path through the seas, and be transformed. For those on a spiritual journey, God is always doing something new by opening a path in the seas of chaos that leads to transformation.

Meditation/Journal: What sea of chaos has the providence of God opened for you on your spiritual journey? What new transformation occurred?

Prayer: O God, your way is through the sea, your path, through the mighty waters; yet your footprints are unseen. In your providence, steer the course of my journey, give me a safe way through the waves, and guide me on the path to your heavenly kingdom, where you live forever and ever. Amen.

Pit in the Path

Scripture: "I cry to God Most High, to God who fulfills his purpose for me. He will send from heaven and save me; he will put to shame those who trample on me. They set a net for my steps; my soul was bowed down. They dug a pit in my path, but they have fallen into it themselves." (Ps 57:2–3, 6)

Reflection: The prayer for help in the passage above from Psalm 57 states that the wicked, who have pursued the pray-er, tried to trap him in a net and even dug a pit in his path. A net is a large piece of material made from threads or ropes knotted and twisted or woven to form a regular pattern with spaces between the threads or ropes. It could be placed on the ground, hidden with leaves, and attached to a bent tree branch or sapling with a trigger, which, when released, would snare whatever had gotten within it by forming a bag around it and raising it above the earth. A pit in a path was another kind of trap. After a deep hole was dug in a well-traveled human or animal path, tree branches with leaves were spread over the pit. Anyone or anything stepping onto the branches would break through, fall into the pit, and not be able to get out. Thus, a pit in a path is a trap. The psalmist acknowledges in thanksgiving that God has shown him mercy and given him refuge from those who sought for unstated reasons to accuse him of something, that is, to trap him. Whatever they were attempting backfired; they fell into the pit they placed in his path. God, who is known for his steadfast love and faithfulness (Ps 57:3b), will fulfill his purpose for the psalmist (Ps 57:2). In one of his speeches, Job says something similar: God "strips understanding from the leaders of the earth, and makes them wander in a pathless waste" (Job 12:24).

God fulfills his purpose for those on a spiritual journey. That is the confidence presented by the psalmist, and that is the confidence required of travelers, who leave order behind and take the path that leads to transformation. As Job makes clear, God saves us, sending the wicked on a pathless waste. Spiritual journeyers need to be aware that nets and pits abound. There are plenty of excuses to stay home to mow the yard, to shovel snow, to take care of the house, to pay the bills, to go to work, to make money, etc. While all those things may be necessary, they are not supreme. The LORD is an adventurer! He is known for steadfast love and faithfulness; he fulfills his purpose for us, he saves us, he removes those who try to trap us, as we fulfill our spiritual purpose. God is our partner, who knows where to find the nets and pits.

Meditation/Journal: As you have journeyed, what pits have you encountered? How has God demonstrated his steadfast love and faithfulness and saved you?

Prayer: I cry to you, God Most High. Be merciful to me and fulfill your purpose for me. Rescue me from the nets set for my steps, and keep me from falling into a pit dug in my path. Wrap me in your steadfast love and faithfulness all the days of my spiritual journey to you. Amen.

Pathway

Scripture: Moses said to the Israelites: "You must therefore be careful to do as the LORD your God has commanded you; you shall not turn to the right or to the left. You must follow exactly the path that the LORD you God has commanded you, so that you may live, and that it may go well with you, and that you may live long in the land that you are to possess." (Deut 5:33–34)

Reflection: A pathway is a route one takes. In his speech to the Israelites, Moses explains God's pathway using the word as a double entendre. It refers to the route the people will take under Joshua's leadership across the Jordan River and into the promised land. But more importantly it also refers to the way of life that God desires for his chosen people. Moses explains that they are to follow a narrow path neither veering to the right or to the left of the 613 commandments that God gives the Israelites. Following this pathway results in life, good luck, and long life in the promised land. In a similar way, the angel sent to Ezra explains the narrow path using the example of a city full of good things set on a plain, "but the entrance to it is narrow and set in a precipitous place, so that there is fire on the right hand and deep water on the left. There is only one path lying between them, that is, between the fire and the water, so that only one person can walk on the path" (2 Esd 7:7–8).

Other biblical authors, like Job, stretches the pathway metaphor, stating that God watches his paths, even setting a bound to the soles of his feet (Job 13:27). Isaiah records the LORD promising to "lead the blind by a road they do not know, by paths they have not known" (Isa 42:16a). The prophet Habakkuk presumes that God walks "along his ancient pathways" (Hab 3:6b), while the OT (A) author of the book of Wisdom compares the unrighteous to an arrow shot at a target; "the air, thus divided, comes together at once, so that no one knows its pathway" (Wis 5:12). Once the call is heard to walk the narrow path of long life before God, one does not know where the path may lead. The Holy One, according to Job, guides and protects the walker, even directing the soles of his or her feet. Some ancient pathways are known only to the LORD, who directs people through transformation into a promised land.

Meditation/Journal: What narrow pathway have you traveled that transformed you? From what did God protect you?

Prayer: O LORD, set a boundary for the soles of my feet that I may never stray to the right or to the left of the life you desire for me. Guide me in your ancient pathways to the fullness of life in your presence forever. Amen.

Straight Path

Scripture: Uzziah said to Judith, "May God grant this to be a perpetual honor to you, and may he reward you with blessings, because you risked your own life when our nation was brought low, and you averted our ruin, walking in the straight path before our God." And all the people said, "Amen. Amen." (Jdt 13:20)

Reflection: Judith is one of very few biblical female warrior heroines. After beheading Holofernes, the Assyrian army commander, she presents his head to Uzziah, the magistrate of Bethulia in Israel. Before Judith acts, Uzziah, the town leaders, and the citizens pray and wait for a deliverer, who happens to be Judith. She leaves behind the orderly life of a woman after hearing God's call. She makes a plan and sets it in motion to rescue her people. In other words, she takes the journey and returns transformed. Uzziah declares her blessed by the Most High God above all other women on earth because she walked the straight path. In the words of the psalmist, her steps held fast to the LORD's paths; her feet did not slip (Ps 17:5). She acknowledged God in all her ways, and he made her ways straight (Prov 3:6). Judith kept straight the path of her feet, and all her ways were sure (Prov 4:26). The LORD led her in the paths of righteousness for his name's sake (Ps 23:3). God's good spirit led Holofernes to her tent on a level path (Ps 143:10), and she dispatched him to beat her enemies and win the praise of her people.

In a similar vein, Tobit teaches his son, Tobias, telling him: "At all times bless the Lord God, and ask him that your ways may be made straight and that all your paths and plans may prosper" (Tob 4:19a). The author of Sirach explains how he sought wisdom openly in his prayer and his feet walked on straight paths (Sir 51:13, 15), whereas the author of Wisdom declares that "the paths of those on earth were set right, and people were taught what pleases [God], and were saved by wisdom" (Wis 9:18). Through the prophet Jeremiah, God promises to lead people "in a straight path in which they shall not stumble" (Jer 31:9b). This is why John the Baptist in the CB (NT) shouts, "Prepare the way of the Lord, make his paths straight" (Mark 1:3; Matt 3:3c; Luke 3:4c). In other words, leave the past, answer the call, take the journey, and be transformed. The author of the Letter to the Hebrews summarizes all this by exhorting his readers to "make straight paths for [their] feet" (Heb 12:13).

Meditation/Journal: What straight path have you taken that brought you home transformed? What order did you leave behind to answer the call?

Prayer: God of Judith, your chosen woman's steps held fast to your paths, and her feet did not slip, as she invoked your name. Grant me the grace to acknowledge you in all my ways and keep my path straight before you today, tomorrow, and forever. Amen.

Bypaths

Scripture: Thus says the LORD, "My people have forgotten me; . . . they have stumbled in their ways, in the ancient roads, and have gone into bypaths, not the highway . . . ." (Jer 18:15)

Reflection: A bypath is a rarely used trail, road, or path, usually located in the country. The prophet Jeremiah narrates that he hears the LORD tell him that his people have taken a detour; they have wondered away, and they are no longer on the major road that he built for them. God laments that his chosen people have fallen into idolatry; they have lost their way by taking a bypath. In other words, they have chosen their own plans. After Jerusalem was destroyed by the Babylonians in 587 BCE, the author of Lamentations alters the bypath image with his response to the suffering Jerusalem experienced. He portrays God as blocking his ways with hewn stones and making his paths crooked (Lam 3:9). In the CB (NT) Acts of the Apostles, Saul (Paul) accuses the magician Elymas of "making crooked the straight paths of the Lord" (Acts 13:10). The magician is on a bypath, and he is trying to guide Saul (Paul) to the same road.

As these and other biblical passages make clear, some people prefer that things remain the same. The order is just fine, even though God keeps calling people to steer clear of the bypath and get on the highway of the journey. Balaam, a HB (OT) prophet, prefers the old order; it takes the angel of the LORD standing in, first, a narrow path and, second, in a narrow place, where there was no way to turn either to the right or to the left, for Balaam's donkey to prophesy to the prophet sitting on his back to hear what God was saying and to take the journey that would lead to his transformation (Num 22:22–35). Balaam was on a bypath; the LORD wanted him on the highway. Balaam thought he was going to curse the Israelites; God had decided that he was going to bless them.

Meditation/Journal: Identify one bypath you have taken during your spiritual journey. Where were you headed? How did God get you back on the highway?

Prayer: O LORD, you are good to those who wait for you and to those who seek you. As I sit quietly listening for your word, keep me from straying on the bypath and keep me on the narrow path of the journey that brings me transformed into your presence. Amen.

Hazardous Path

Scripture: "[The wicked] are thrust into a net by their own feet, and they walk into a pitfall. A trap seizes them by the heel; a snare lays hold of them. A rope is hid for them in the ground, a trap for them in the path." (Job 18:8–10)

Reflection: In one of his speeches to Job, Bildad the Shuhite declares Job to be among the wicked who get trapped in their own schemes. Bildad states that the wicked walk right into the net they set or the pit they dug. They step into the trap they set and are held in it. Like a rope covered in soil which grabs them when they trip it, they walk a hazardous path. Some of the psalms state that the arrogant hide traps (Pss 140:5; 141:9–10; 142:3b), making the journey hazardous for the just. Indeed, Job responds to Bildad's words by explaining that God is hunting him. He states that God "has walled up [his] way so that [he] cannot pass, and he has set darkness upon [his] paths" (Job 19:8); Job seems to be stumbling in the dark. In his farewell speech, Jacob describes his son Dan as being like "a snake by the roadside, a viper along the path, that bites the horse's heels so that its rider falls backward" (Gen 49:17). In other words, the tribe of Dan is good at covert warfare, unhorsing enemies, like a snake biting a horse's hoof and causing it to throw off its rider. Dan is a hazardous path for his tribe's enemies.

Those who travel hazardous paths need wisdom, states Sirach. " . . . [S]he will walk with them on tortuous paths; she will bring fear and dread upon them, and will torment them by her discipline until she trusts them, and she will test them with her ordinances" (Sir 4:17). Life's trials discipline a person and teach wisdom. Such wisdom instructs one not to follow every path (Sir 5:9), not to take a path full of hazards, not to stumble over an obstacle twice (Sir 32:20), not to be overconfident on a smooth road, and to give good heed to the paths one chooses to walk (Sir 32:21–22). According to Wisdom, it is easy to stray on the hazardous path of error (Wis 12:24).

Meditation/Journal: What hazardous path have you traveled? What wisdom did you acquire by walking it? What did you learn from your mistakes?

Prayer: O GOD, my Lord, I turn my eyes to you, for I seek refuge in you. Protect me from all hazardous traps during my lifetime journey. Fill me with the wisdom of the Spirit that my path may take me directly into your presence forever. Amen.

Thorns on the Path

Scripture: "The earth shall be left desolate, and its fields shall be plowed up, and its roads and all its paths shall bring forth thorns, because no sheep will go along them." (2 Esd 16:32)

Reflection: The words spoken by God in Second Esdras, chapters 15 and 16, are based on the belief that the world is coming to an end soon. Such literature is written at a time of crises; it is designed to give hope to believers by narrating the destruction of nonbelievers as a result of their refusal to repent. The image of thorns on the path is borrowed from the prophet Isaiah, who, after recording the love-song for the vineyard that produces only wild grapes, declares that the vineyard will become a waste, "overgrown with briers and thorns" (Isa 5:6a). Later, the same prophet records, "On that day every place where there used to be a thousand vines . . . will become briers and thorns" (Isa 7:23). While Isaiah has in mind the destruction of Jerusalem at the hand of the Babylonians, the word *thorns* conveys the negativity associated with abandonment, destruction, and wilderness.

In his parable about four types of seeds, Jesus employs the image of thorns on the path to describe those in spiritual exile. He states that the first type of seed "fell on the path, and the birds came and ate it up" (Mark 4:4; cf. Matt 13:4; Luke 8:5), while the third type of seed "fell among thorns, and the thorns grew up and choked it, and it yielded no grain" (Mark 4:7; cf. Matt 13:7; Luke 8:7). In the interpretation that follows the parable, the author explains: "The sower sows the word. These are the ones on the path where the word is sown: when they hear, Satan immediately comes and takes away the word that is sown in them. And others are those sown among the thorns: these are the ones who hear the word, but the cares of the world, and the lure of wealth, and the desire for other things come in and choke the word, and it yields nothing" (Mark 4:14–15, 18–19; cf. Matt 13:19, 22; Luke 8:11–12, 14). On the spiritual journey, walkers should take care that the word planted in their hearts is not lost, stolen, or trampled; otherwise, they have no faith. Likewise, those on the spiritual journey should beware of thorns on the path which replace the word they hear with cares, riches, and pleasures of life; otherwise, they discover that they are this worldly and not other worldly. In other words, traveling the spiritual path can result in reverse transformation; journeyers discover that they have returned to the old order instead of leaving it behind and being transformed into the new order.

Meditation/Journal: As you journey, when have you discovered yourself lost on the path or choked by thorns? What did you do to get moving again to transformation?

Prayer: God of transformation, you spread your word on my path of life. Grant me the grace to hear it deeply in my heart so that it roots and grows in me. Help me to recognize the cares, riches, and pleasures of life that can choke your word. Hear my prayer through your Word, Jesus Christ. Amen.

Mount of Olives Path

Scripture: "[Two disciples] brought [the colt] to Jesus; and after throwing their cloaks on the colt, they set Jesus on it. As he rode along, people kept spreading their cloaks on the road. As he was now approaching the path down from the Mount of Olives, the whole multitude of the disciples began to praise God joyfully with a loud voice for all the deeds of power that they had seen . . . . " (Luke 19:35–37)

Reflection: All four gospels mention the Mount of Olives several times (Mark 11:1, 13:3, 14:26; Matt 21:1, 24:3, 26:30; Luke 19:29, 21:37, 22:39; John 8:1), but only the author of Luke's Gospel mentions the path down from it. Otherwise known as Mount Scopus, the biblical name indicates that a large number of olive trees once grew on the mountain's slopes. This place of prayer opposite Jerusalem is where the synoptic gospels (Mark, Matthew, Luke) place Jesus beginning his triumphal entry into Jerusalem echoing words of the prophet Zechariah (9:9). It is also where he is arrested after experiencing unique Lukan agony (22:44), and from which he, again uniquely Lukan, ascends into heaven (Acts 1:11–12). For the author of the third gospel, the unique mention of the path down from the Mount of Olives serves to reinforce the journey theme employed by the author (Luke 2:41–51, 9:3, 51, 13:22, 17:11).

Jesus leaves behind the Jewish order of his day because he hears the call to announce the presence of the kingdom of God. After preparing for his mission, he was baptized and tempted by the devil in the wilderness. Because he was full of the Holy Spirit's power from the moment of his conception, he embraced the journey to Jerusalem, where, after dying, being raised from the dead (being transformed), and ascending into heaven, he continued the path of transformation to become a model for others who travel the path down from the Mount of Olives and back up it again. In other words, his triumphal entry into Jerusalem down from the Mount of Olives brought him to suffering, death, and resurrection, and led him back up to the Mount of Olives for his ascension—transformation—into heaven.

Meditation/Journal: What experience in your life began as a journey down a path that you ended by going up the path again after being transformed?

Prayer: Blessed is your Son, who comes in your name, O LORD. He brings peace from heaven and glory from you. Trace in me the way of his path that the steps down of my lifetime journey may take me up spiritually transformed into your presence. Amen.

Stream by the Path

Scripture: "The LORD says to my lord, 'Sit at my right hand until I make your enemies your footstool.' The LORD sends out from Zion your mighty scepter. Rule in the midst of your foes. [You] will drink from the stream by the path; therefore [you] will lift up [your] head." (Ps 110:1–2, 7)

Reflection: Psalm 110 is best classified as a royal song sung at the coronation of Judean kings. Since the LORD is the supreme king of the Israelites, he instructs the human king to sit at his right hand, the position of power. Thus, the king becomes second in command. God even subdues the king's enemies, spreading his reign from Mount Zion (the Temple) outward over his foes. In other words, the LORD promises the king that he will deliver him from all his foes. He can stop to drink from the stream that flows by the path he takes to win battles, and there he will be refreshed. The stream by the path functions as a double entendre; it can refer to liquid refreshment consumed by the king, and it can refer to the grace with which God endows his chosen king to rule his chosen people.

The importance of a stream by the path in biblical literature is often missed by those who are used to turning on the faucet to get fresh and clean water. However, for those who lived in the rugged land and arid climate of Israel, a stream by the path signifies refreshment and life. One characteristic of the promised land is that it contains flowing streams (Deut 8:7), which cause trees to produce fruits (Ps 1:3), for which the deer long (Ps 42:1), which gladden the city of God (Ps 46:4), and by which birds of the air live and sing (Ps 104:12). In other words, the stream near the path sustains God's creatures, including the king, giving them life and grace. According to the book of Proverbs, a gushing stream is a sign of wisdom (Prov 18:4). The prophet Isaiah contains the LORD's promise to extend prosperity to Jerusalem and to make the wealth of nations coming to her like an overflowing stream (Isa 66:12b). The stream by the path for those who answer the call to leave order behind and take the journey results in transformation for those who drink from it and lift up their heads.

Meditation/Journal: What stream have you discovered flowing near the path you have taken? What kind of new life did you receive when drinking from it?

Prayer: Like the deer who longs for flowing streams, so do I long for you, my God. I thirst for you, the living God. Give me the grace that strengthens me on the path of transformation so that I never cease to praise you, my help and my God, forever. Amen.

4

Route, Highway, Gateway

Promised Land Route

Scripture: Moses said to the Israelites: "All of you came to me and said, 'Let us send men ahead of us to explore the land for us and bring back a report to us regarding the route by which we should go up and the cities we will come to.' The plan seemed good to me, and I selected twelve of you, one from each tribe." (Deut 1:22–23)

Reflection: The book of Deuteronomy portrays Moses addressing the Israelites before invading the promised land. On the east side of the Jordan River, Moses tells the people, "See, the LORD your God has given the land to you; go up, take possession, as the LORD, the God of your ancestors, has promised you; do not fear or be dismayed" (Deut 1:21). He reminds his audience that they had requested that he send out scouts in advance to determine what route would be best to take. Moses did as was requested: he selected one man from each of the twelve tribes to reconnoiter the land in preparation for the journey into it. In a similar way, the prophet Ezra records the word of the Lord telling him: "Surely it was I who brought you through the sea, and made safe highways for you where there was no road; I gave you Moses as leader and Aaron as priest" (2 Esdras 1:13).

After the order of wandering in the desert for forty years, Moses reminds the Israelites that their call is to cross the Jordan into the land promised by God to Abraham and Sarah and their descendants. As the people note, they need to prepare to answer that call by sending scouts to determine the best way to make the journey of claiming what God had promised hundreds of years before. The spies gathered produce from the land and reported that the land was good (Deut 1:24–25). But the people were not yet ready to take the journey; they needed further encouragement from Moses and more won battles with enemies before they were prepared to march into the promised land. However, throughout their preparation period, the LORD was transforming them from fear to courage, from citizen to soldier, and from tribes to nation. When the transformation was complete, they took the route indicated into the promised land. After Moses died, they were led by Joshua. They came home to the land given to their ancestors hundreds of years before, and they were transformed.

Meditation/Journal: When have you left an ordered life after hearing God's call, prepared yourself to answer it, but stopped for some reason before making the journey that led to transformation? Why did you pause?

Prayer: LORD, you promise me glorious transformation in the land to which you lead me. Remove my fear and replace it with the courage I need to answer your call by taking the highway of transformation to you, who have promised me life eternal. Amen.

Caravan Route

Scripture: "Now Zebah and Zalmunna [, kings of Midian, enemies of Israel,] were . . . with their army, about fifteen thousand men, all who were left of all the army of the people of the east; for one hundred twenty thousand men bearing arms had fallen. So Gideon went up by the caravan route . . . and attacked the army; for the army was off its guard." (Judg 8:10–11)

Reflection: The book of Judges is built on a recurring pattern: Israel is disloyal to God, Israel is oppressed by her enemies, Israel repents and cries to God for help, God sends a deliverer. While some of the tales following the pattern are short, other stories are much longer. Such a long story is the one about Gideon (Judg 6:1—8:35). This military commander is called by God to drive from the land the Midianites, who stole food and livestock and destroyed crops. In the part of the story narrated above, Gideon defeats the Midianite kings by not taking the direct route to where they are camped. He had already decimated their forces, but they retreated. He circles around them, taking the caravan route, otherwise known as the route of those who live in tents watching their flocks. Using the element of surprise, after passing through the nomadic campsite, Gideon captures the enemy leaders and kills them in retaliation for them having killed his brothers.

In this short account of a much longer narrative, the caravan route proves beneficial to Gideon but lethal to the kings of Midian. In the book of Deuteronomy, Moses reminds the Israelites that while God directed them to take the route of the wilderness of Moab (Deut 2:8b), they were also instructed not to engage in battle with the Moabites. Isaiah reports that after the defeat of Judah by Babylon, the highways were deserted; travelers had quit the road because it was too dangerous (Isa 33:8). Tobit reports that during the reign of Sennacherib, the highways into Media were unsafe to travel (Tob 1:15). The author of the First Book of Maccabees reports that Judas Maccabeus often ambushed the enemies of the Jews on the highways (1 Macc 5:4). In other words, once one hears the call to leave the order of the world behind to journey, the route of transformation may contain dangers along the way. Sometimes one can take the caravan route to skirt the dangers, but other times one must travel the wilderness route, trusting in divine protection.

Meditation/Journal: When have you most recently traveled the safe route to transformation? When have you traveled the dangerous route to transformation?

Prayer: Almighty God, you give protection to those who answer your call and embrace the route upon which you set their feet. Make safe my journey on dangerous routes until I am transformed before you. Amen.

King's Highway

Scripture: "Moses sent messengers . . . to the king of Edom, . . . 'Now let us pass through your land. We will not pass through field or vineyard, or drink water from any well; we will go along the King's Highway, not turning aside to the right hand or to the left until we have passed through your territory.'" (Num 20:14, 17)

Reflection: Even with the assurance given by Moses to the king of Edom that the Israelites would not trample fields, take grapes from vineyards, or draw water to drink from wells, the king of Edom would not let the Israelites pass over the King's Highway. They even promised to stay on the highway, and, if they or their livestock drank any water, they promised to pay him for it. But he will not permit them to pass through (Num 20:18–21). The King's Highway was a trade route of the ancient world; it connected Africa with Mesopotamia, running from Heliopolis, Egypt, eastward to Aqaba in the Sinai desert, then northward through Edom, Moab, and Ammon to Damascus, then northeast to Resafa on the Euphrates River. Whoever controlled the highway also controlled the trade. When requesting the right of way of the king of Edom, the Israelites were interrupting the flow of trade into and out of his kingdom.

Trade is still important at journey destinations be they religious or otherwise. There are always shops selling mementos of the place. Religiously, one can purchase candles, books, medals, etc. Secularly, one can buy a T-shirt, a spoon, a keychain, etc. In either case, there are usually carts or shops selling food. The lesson here is not not engaging in trade; the lesson is to respect other's property while continuing a journey. The Israelites promised not to trample fields, not to eat grapes from vineyards, and not to drink water from wells belonging to the Edomites. While they had left their ordered lives in Egypt behind to answer the call they heard from God through Moses, they were prepared to continue their journey without destroying the land through which they wanted to travel to get to the promised land. In other words, their transformation was delayed, as they had to figure out a different route to get to the promised land. When passing through another's territory—on the sidewalk, on the street, on the interstate, etc.—we should be respectful of others' property so that trade flourishes while the journey continues.

Meditation/Journal: Specifically name the ways you respect the property of others while continuing your lifetime journey? How do others demonstrate their respect for your property?

Prayer: Grant that all the highways I travel lead to you, O God. Make me aware of all the lands through which I journey, and give me a deep respect for the property of others throughout the transformation you bring about in me. All praise be yours now and forever. Amen.

Blood on the Highway

Scripture: " . . . Joab [, the commander of King David's forces,] took Amasa [, the commander of the army appointed by rebellious Absalom, David's son,] by the beard with his right hand to kiss him. But Amasa did not notice the sword in Joab's hand; Joab struck him in the belly so that his entrails poured out on the ground, and he died. Amasa lay wallowing in his blood on the highway, and [one of Joab's men] saw that all the people were stopping. Since he saw that all who came by him were stopping, he carried Amasa from the highway into a field, and threw a garment over him." (2 Sam 20:9b–10a, 12)

Reflection: The account of revolt within the ranks of David's army and the slaying of those who led it is not a story one will hear in Sunday school, nor will it serve as the basis for a sermon! Just sorting one character from another is quite a task for those not familiar with the Second Book of Samuel in the HB (OT). Joab, David's army commander, finds Amasa, who had been appointed army commander by David's Son, Absalom, and slays him because he had delayed following the king's order to summon the men of Judah to find the scoundrel Sheba, who had incited the people of Israel to withdraw from David (2 Sam 20:1–5). In other words, Amasa was less than loyal. One of Joab's men saw Amasa surrounded by blood on the highway and took him to a field, where he covered him, out of respect for the blood.

Not only were the days of biblical kingship bloody, but, ironically, blood was considered to be the life of the living being, even when it was poured on the highway. Life is given by God, and all blood must be returned to God. Joab, who previously killed Abner (2 Sam 3:26–30), not only sought revenge for all the trouble Absalom caused, but he cleared the field of those who were not 100 percent loyal to King David. In Luke's Gospel, Jesus tells a parable about Jewish blood shed on the road from Jerusalem to Jericho. Both a Jewish priest and a Jewish Levite see the bloodied man and walk by. However, a Samaritan, much like Joab's soldier, stops to show respect for the blood and discovers that the man is alive. So, he bandaged his wounds, took him to an inn, and paid for his stay there (Luke 10:29–37). On our lifetime journey, we may discover blood on the highway as the result of car accidents involving people and people or people and animals. Blood on the highway may be the result of deep arguments or litter tossed on a city street. Those who clean the blood on the highway demonstrate great respect not only to those whose blood was shed, but also to the God who gives life to those who journey through the world.

Meditation/Journal: During your lifetime journey, where have you found blood on the highway? How did you show respect for the life that was in the blood?

Prayer: Creator God, you bestow life in the blood in everything you have created. When it falls on the highway, it cries out to you to be covered with respect. Grant me a deeper awareness of all the blood on the highway of life I journey, and a deeper respect for all you have created. Amen.

Highway to the Fuller's Field

Scripture: "The king of Assyria sent the Tartan, the Rabsaris, and the Rabshakeh with a great army . . . to King Hezekiah at Jerusalem. They went up and came to Jerusalem. When they arrived, they came and stood by the conduit of the upper pool, which is on the highway to the Fuller's Field." (2 Kgs 18:17).

Reflection: Sennacherib, king of Assyria, invaded Judah in 701 BCE and forced Hezekiah of Judah to pay a large tribute of silver and gold to him.

The Tartan, the Rabsaris, and the Rabshakeh—titles given to Assyrian military officers—travel to Jerusalem to deliver Sennacherib's message about not being able to defeat his army to Hezekiah. The prophet Isaiah contains a slightly different version of this account, but in the same place, that is, on the highway to the Fuller's Field (Isa 36:2), which is also mentioned in Isaiah 7:3. Thus, this highway was a well-known landmark in Jerusalem at the time of the monarchy. Because the fuller needed access to plenty of water to clean, whiten, bleach, thicken, shrink, or dye cloth, his shop was located near a water conduit emptying into a pool or a conduit flowing from a pool. After washing the cloth, the fuller spread it out on the ground to dry and to be bleached by the sun. This place designated for professional laundering and cleaning services became a metaphor for purity (Ps 51:7; Jer 2:22, 4:14; Zech 3:3–5; Rev 4:4). That is why the Markan description of Jesus' clothes at his transfiguration describes them as becoming "dazzling white, such as no one [fuller] on earth could bleach them" (Mark 9:3).

Biblical writers speculate as to where this then-well-known place might have been. Many people took the highway to the Fuller's Field to obtain the services of a person who knew how to clean, whiten, bleach, thicken, shrink, or dye cloth. In other words, it was like a familiar interstate highway, road, or street. Often, people hear God's call to walk the highway of the familiar, but to do so with deeper awareness or perspective. Paying attention may be all the preparation that is necessary to take a journey on the highway to the Fuller's Field. While on the way home, a person may recognize that he or she became attuned to God's presence, reached a solution to a problem, or encountered beauty where it had not been embraced before. In other words, one was transformed, like Hezekiah was transformed by Isaiah's words: "Thus says the LORD: Do not be afraid because of the words that you have heard, with which the servants of the King of Assyria have reviled me. I myself will put a spirit in him, so that he shall hear a rumor and return to his own land . . . " (2 Kgs 19:6–7). And that is exactly what occurred.

Meditation/Journal: What visit to a familiar place most recently transformed you? What awareness or new perspective brought this about?

Prayer: O LORD, enthroned above the heavens, you are God, you alone, of all the kingdoms of the earth. Open my ears and eyes that I may hear your word and see your works and be transformed on this familiar journey today, tomorrow, and forever. Amen.

ROUTE, HIGHWAY, GATEWAY

Highways to Zion

Scripture: "Happy are those whose strength is in you [, O LORD,] in whose heart are the highways to Zion. As they go through the valley . . . they make it a place of springs; the early rain also covers it with pools. They go from strength to strength; the God of gods will be seen in Zion." (Ps 84:5–7)

Reflection: Psalm 84 is a journey song; it was sung by pilgrims as they walked towards Jerusalem to visit the Temple, the lovely dwelling place of the LORD (Ps 84:1). As the psalm progresses, the singers recount sparrows and swallows who build nests and hatch young on the Temple's ledges; the birds are described as being happy because they live in God's house, where they sing his praises (Ps 84:3–4). Happier are those whose strength for the journey comes from God, who inspires their hearts to travel the highway to Zion, the hill upon which Jerusalem was built, to see the God of gods in his Temple there (Ps 84:7). After Jerusalem and the Temple were destroyed by the Babylonians in 587 BCE, the prophet Jeremiah proclaimed her restoration to all her deported citizens: "Set up road markers for yourself, make yourself guideposts; consider well the highway, the road by which you went. Return, O virgin Israel, return to these your cities" (Jer 31:21). Using the highway image, Jeremiah urged Jerusalem's citizens not to forget the highway to God inscribed in their hearts. They needed to erect road signs so they would not get lost.

As the psalm makes clear, the highway to Jerusalem is found in the heart. God strengthens the pilgrim to leave the old ordered life behind and to answer the call issued by the psalmist to make the journey to Jerusalem's Temple on Zion, where he or she will see God. The result will be a transforming experience both by making the journey and by presenting himself or herself face to face with God in the Temple courts. What awaits the traveler on Zion is the opportunity for the LORD to hear directly his or her prayer (Ps 84:8). One day on Zion, functioning as a doorkeeper, is better than a thousand spent in other places (Ps 84:10). The LORD is the source of hearing the call, leaving all behind, taking the journey, and being transformed. The psalmist declares him to be like the sun, the source of all living things, and like a shield that protects (Ps 84:11a). Favor, honor, and all good things are bestowed by God upon those who walk uprightly on the journey, trusting the God of gods in Zion (Ps 84:11b–12). In their hearts are traced the highways to Zion, the highway to God, the highway to transformation.

Meditation/Journal: Is there a highway to God inscribed in your heart? To where has that road taken you? What transformation was wrought in you by taking the journey?

Prayer: While your presence fills the universe, O LORD, you choose to dwell in temples made by human hands to which people come to sing for joy to you, the living God. In my heart trace the road that leads to you and give me the strength to make the journey in response to your call. I trust that you will answer my prayer and bring me transformed into your presence. Amen.

Highway to/from Assyria and Egypt

Scripture: "On that day there will be a highway from Egypt to Assyria, and the Assyrians will come into Egypt, and the Egyptians into Assyria, and the Egyptians will worship with the Assyrians. On that day Israel will be the third with Egypt and Assyria, a blessing in the midst of the earth, whom the LORD of hosts has blessed, saying, 'Blessed be Egypt my people, and Assyria the work of my hands, and Israel my heritage.'" (Isa 19:23–25)

Reflection: The prophet Isaiah dreams of a future universalism in the three verses quoted above. Israel would share its knowledge of God with Egyptians and Assyrians, and those three countries would be one in faith. The unity would be enabled with a highway that stretched from Assyria—through Jerusalem—to Egypt. The road, which would enable trade, would unite all people around the LORD. This idea is often expressed biblically as nations streaming to God (Pss 67:2; 72:11, 17; 113:4; Isa 55:5, 66:18; Jer 3:17; Mal 3:12). While the position of tiny Israel is exaggerated as being a blessing when compared to large Egypt and large Assyria, Isaiah suggests a day when Egypt and Assyria will be agents of the LORD. Needless to say, Isaiah's dream is big, especially when the reader considers that both Assyria and Egypt are Israel's enemies! Assyria defeated the northern kingdom of Israel in 722 BCE, and before that, from 1630–1230 BCE, the Hebrews were captives in Egypt. Furthermore, the Israelites would find it impossible to hear God declare the first two of the following beatitudes: "Blessed be Egypt my people, and Assyria the work of my hands, and Israel my heritage" (Isa

19:25). Earlier, in less explosive language, the prophet Isaiah declared that there would "be a highway from Assyria for the remnant that is left of [the LORD's] people, as there was for Israel when they came up from the land of Egypt" (Isa 11:16). The highway would lead to Jerusalem.

Isaiah's dream of one highway uniting enemy people remains a dream. A country may be made of many states—like the United States of America or the United States of Mexico—but countries still fight over borders and invade each other to subjugate people and their economies. Modern highways enable some—not all—people the opportunity to journey to another country and be transformed in the process. Air travel is now a highway that can unite enemies. Ships travel highways through the oceans to unite enemies. The telephone enables enemies to speak to each other about diplomacy instead of declaring war. And maybe the greatest highway of modern time that enables communicative connections between others is the internet. While Isaiah's dream never materialized during his time, maybe modern people can make it a reality.

Meditation/Journal: What highway do you use the most? What transformation occurs as a result of your journey on it?

Prayer: O God, let all the peoples of the earth praise you! May your way be known by all. May your saving power be revealed to all nations. Grant that all nations be blessed in you and united as one, as a highway connects one country to another. Blessed be you, O LORD, who alone does marvelous things. Amen.

Holy Highway

Scripture: "A highway shall be [in the wilderness], and it shall be called the Holy Way; the unclean shall not travel on it, but it shall be for God's people; no traveler, not even fools, shall go astray." (Isa 35:8)

Reflection: By the middle of the seventh century BCE, Isaiah is offering hope to Israel and Judah using contrasting imagery. In chapter 35, the prophet contrasts the wilderness with the blossoming of wild flowers; not only will the barren and abandoned territory burst into bloom, but all will be fertile with life. The dry land will see the glory of the LORD (Isa 35:2), who comes to save his people (Isa 35:4d). The contrasts continue with blind eyes seeing, deaf ears hearing, lame feet leaping, and dumb tongues speaking and singing (Isa 35:5–6). Water will flow in the wilderness; along the streams reeds and rushes will grow (Isa 35:6b–7). The highway through the wilderness will bring survivors to Jerusalem. The scattered people will have a way to return to their homeland. Nothing will afflict them on their way home (Isa 35:9). Only those whom God has redeemed shall travel that Holy Way (Isa 35:9b). As stated by Isaiah: "And the ransomed of the LORD shall return, and come to Zion with singing; everlasting joy shall be upon their heads; they shall obtain joy and gladness, and sorrow and sighing shall flee away" (Isa 35:10). The transformation of the land of Israel is presented in contrast to the transformation of the landscape of its enemy in chapter 34. In other words, the Holy Way brings the Israelites back to their land, just like their previous journey from Egypt once did.

The Holy Way or path of holiness results in transformation. Only the purified, chastened, redeemed, and transformed people of God can travel the highway. No traveler, no mentally-challenged person will get lost on the path of holiness. God's people are seeing, hearing, and speaking about their divine teacher, who keeps them from turning either to the right or to the left off the Holy Way. This is the same teacher, who calls people today to leave the old order behind and prepare to take the journey urged by the Spirit. It will be full of contrasts that lead to personal transformation, and, if a member of a group, community transformation. Those who complete the journey of transformation are found singing in everlasting joy and gladness. They have seen the glory of the LORD, the majesty of God.

Meditation/Journal: What Holy Way have you most recently traveled? What old order did you leave behind? What call did you hear? How did you prepare? What transformation occurred in you?

Prayer: LORD God, open my blind eyes, clear my deaf ears, heal my lame legs, and loosen my dumb tongue that I may sing with joy and gladness your praise as I journey your Holy Way. Grant that your path of holiness may result in my transformation today, tomorrow, and forever. Amen.

Highway for God

Scripture: "A voice cries out: 'In the wilderness prepare the way of the LORD, make straight in the desert a highway for our God.'" (Isa 40:3)

Reflection: Previous entries were about the highway for people to travel. In chapter 40, Isaiah introduces the motif of the LORD needing a highway upon which to travel (Isa 49:11). God's highway will be level; every valley will be raised, and every mountain and hill will be leveled. The uneven ground and rough places in the road will be smoothed (Isa 40:4). God's highway, of course, leads to Jerusalem, where his glory will be revealed, and his people shall see it together in his Temple (Isa 40:5). God's highway leads his scattered and captive people home to Jerusalem, who is instructed by the prophet to ascend the highest mountain and shout, "Here is your God!" (Isa 40:9c) The Lord GOD is coming to Jerusalem with power, and all should know it, according to Isaiah. The prophet employs the metaphor of empire building. A highway is essential to build a kingdom. The road is used to transport the military, to facilitate trade both within and without the country. The highway is the means of communication. The stage direction given to Jerusalem to shout that God is coming is comparable to the messenger shouting that God, the emperor supreme, is on the way.

That same metaphor is employed by the author of Mark's Gospel who quotes Isaiah 40:3 and applies it to John the Baptist preparing the way for Jesus, the Son of God, whose ministry was proclaiming the kingdom or empire of God (Mark 1:3, 15; cf. Matt 3:3, 4:17). The author of Matthew's Gospel even presents John the Baptist proclaiming the kingdom of God before Jesus does (Matt 3:2). The author of Luke's Gospel enhances the quotation from Isaiah by including verse 4 and rewriting it with the alternate words in brackets: "Every valley shall be lifted up [filled], and every mountain and hill [shall] be made low; the uneven ground shall become level [and the crooked shall be made straight], and the rough places [ways] a plain [made smooth]" (Isa 40:4; Luke 3:5). Luke adds: "and all flesh shall see the salvation of God" (Luke 3:6; cf. Isa 40:5). The Lukan Jesus repeatedly proclaims the coming of the kingdom of God (Luke 4:43; 8:1; 9:11, 60; 10:9, 11; 11:20; 12:32; 17:20–21; 21:31). In other words, God in the person of Jesus of Nazareth is here. Hearing his call to follow means leaving one's previous kingdom behind and taking the journey to Jerusalem. The result is transformation through death to new life.

Meditation/Journal: What type of highway have you built for God? How did he come to you? How did you announce his coming or arrival?

Prayer: O LORD, in the wilderness of my life I prepare a highway for you. Raise up the valleys of my despair, lower the mountains of my pride, and level the roughness of my attitude. Let your glory be revealed through me during my lifetime journey, so that others may see it and praise your name now and forever. Amen.

Gateway

Scripture: "When [the hand of the LORD] brought me [, Ezekiel, to the site of the first Temple in Jerusalem], a man was there, whose appearance shone like bronze, with a linen cord and a measuring reed in his hand; and he was standing in the gateway. Then he went into the gateway facing east, going up its steps, and measured the threshold of the gate, one reed deep. Then he measured the inner vestibule of the gateway, one cubit. Then he measured the vestibule of the gateway, eight cubits . . . . Then he measured the width of the opening of the gateway, ten cubits; and the width of the gateway, thirteen cubits." (Ezek 40:3, 6, 8–9, 11)

Reflection: In Ezekiel's vision, narrated in chapter 40 of his prophetic book, he writes about the dimensions of the temple structures which begin at the gateway, the main entrance facing east toward the sun. A gateway is a road through a wall; it is an entryway into something, such as a walled city or the Temple. Because the gateway was the weakest point, it was as thick as the wall with its depth usually lengthened and towers added. Some gateways opened to a small chamber (vestibule), which possessed another gateway. The corridor leading from one gateway to another might contain guardrooms. Gateways both kept people out and kept people in; they kept enemies out, and they provided protection to citizens within. Because gateways were public places, communal activities occurred there. Public assemblies took place at gateways, along with the public market. Hospitality to the stranger was extended at the gateway (Gen 19:1); it was the place where the elders sat and where legal authentication occurred for documents requiring witnesses. Even executions took place near the gateway (2 Sam 3:27). The east gateway of the Temple for Ezekiel is the entrance to the holy place where one can meet God (Ezek 8:3; 11:1).

Those on a journey pass through many gateways. Store fronts with tall facades and automatic opening and closing glass doors are gateways to food, hardware, and clothes. The large double doors of malls are gateways to public areas, food courts, and information booths. Storm doors and/or brightly-painted front doors on homes along a street serve as gateways for those who live in them and for those who come to visit. Even the canopies over side doors of churches are gateways for those who drive under them to drop off worshippers. Journeyers leave the old order of life behind to prepare themselves to answer God's call to make the trip through whatever gateways they may pass. As they move through those gateways, they are transformed again and again.

Meditation/Journal: Through what gateway have you most recently passed? What transformation—no matter how minor—occurred in you as a result?

Prayer: All praise is due to you, O God. I am awed by the signs of your presence. The gateways of the morning and the evening bring joy to my heart. Guide the footsteps of my journey through the gateways of transformation with your Holy Spirit. In your mercy, hear my prayer. Amen.

5

Walk

God Walks

Scripture: "[The man and the woman] heard the sound of the LORD God walking in the garden at the time of the evening breeze, and the man and his wife hid themselves from the presence of the LORD God among the trees of the garden. But the LORD God called to the man, and said to him, 'Where are you?' He said, 'I heard the sound of you in the garden, and I was afraid, because I was naked; and I hid myself.'" (Gen 3:8–10)

Reflection: The best simple journey is to take a walk in the garden. According to the book of Genesis, even God likes to walk in the garden while the evening breeze cools him. God has a close relationship with what he created. However, his closeness to creation is contrasted with the man's and woman's desire for distance, hiding themselves from their Creator! God's desire to journey through the garden to be close to all he made stands against the naked couple desiring to conceal themselves behind trees, shrubs, and other plants. They have decided not to walk with God in the garden. In a similar motif, there is the apocryphal story of Susanna, who at noon used to go into "her husband's garden to walk" (Sus 1:7 [Dan 13:7]). Susanna is like God walking in the garden, where two elders saw her, "going in and walking about" (Sus 1:8 [Dan 13:8]), and they began to lust for her. If she did not sleep with them, they told her that they would lie about her sleeping with a young man. They testified: "While we were walking in the garden alone, this woman came in with two maids, shut the garden doors, and dismissed the maids. Then a young man, who was hiding there, came to her and lay with her" (Sus 1:36–37 [Dan 13:36–37]). The two elders, snakes in the garden, lie to the people, who condemn her to death until God stirs the holy spirit of a young man named Daniel, who proves them wrong and sets Susanna free. Thus, the hidden condemnation that took place in the garden through the words of the elders is contrasted to the revealed acquittal that occurs there through the interrogation of Daniel, whose name means "God judges"!

One takes a walk in a garden (conservation area, field, park, etc.) because it is sacred space. It is a place of life and tranquility. God wants to walk with people in a garden, protected by an ancient wall, a modern fence, or a rock border. A garden is a place that is different from ordinary life. While yards may contain flowering plants and lots of green grass, a garden reveals paths that twist and turn through life. A person leaves the order of the street traffic to journey through a garden early in the morning, during his or her lunch break, or after work. In a garden, we can hear God's call, just like the first man did, and answer—not by hiding—with a response to keep on traveling through the garden of life to transformation, because we decide to walk with God in the garden.

Meditation/Journal: When was the last time you took a walk through a garden of any kind? What made you aware of God's presence there? What call did you hear?

Prayer: O eternal God, you know all that is secret, and you are aware of all things before they come to be. Guide my steps through the garden of life, enable me to hear your call, and keep me safe on my walk of transformation every day of my life. Amen.

Abraham and Isaac Walk

Scripture: "Abraham took the wood of the burnt offering and laid it on his son Isaac, and he himself carried the fire and the knife. So the two of them walked on together. Isaac said to his father Abraham, 'Father!' And he said, 'Here I am, my son.' He said, 'The fire and the wood are here, but where is the lamb for a burnt offering?' Abraham said, 'God himself will provide the lamb for a burnt offering, my son.' So the two of them walked on together." (Gen 22:6–8)

Reflection: Abraham thinks that he is on a walk to the land of Moriah to sacrifice his son, Isaac. Abraham has left behind the order of his camp after hearing God's call to take his beloved son to a mountain, yet to be revealed, and offer him to God as a burnt offering (Gen 22:1–2). Abraham prepares for and makes the journey. Isaac thinks that they are leaving camp in answer to God's call to offer a lamb for a burnt offering to God. Isaac has no idea that his father believes that he is the lamb for the burnt offering. The narrator of the story tells us two times that they walked on together each with his own presupposition of what was going to take place. Just as Abraham was about to complete the reason for his journey—slaughtering Isaac—and Isaac becomes aware of who the burnt offering is, the angel of the LORD transforms both of them. Abraham's hand with the knife is stopped, and Isaac, who is as good as dead, is given back his life. Just as the two of them have walked on together to Moriah, now they walk on together transformed by the experiences of the journey.

Like Abraham and Isaac, we usually do not know to where the journey may take us. We hear the call, like Abraham and Isaac, to walk with another to somewhere we have never been before. It may be a call to walk through abuse, grief, or disease. We answer by preparing ourselves as best we can, and then we take the journey, not knowing where we go until we get there. God promises to let us know when we have arrived. The result of the walk with another is transformation. No one can walk with another human being through abuse of any kind and not be transformed by the experience. No one can walk with another through grief and not be changed by the sadness of loss. Supporting a friend with cancer, an amputation, or serious surgery leaves us transformed. The two people have walked on together, and both of them have been altered by the journey.

Meditation/Journey: With whom have you walked recently? What order did you leave behind? How did you hear the call to take the walk? Where did the journey take you? How were you transformed?

Prayer: God of Abraham and Isaac, open my ears to hear your call to walk on together with another. Strengthen my will, guide my preparation, lead me on the journey, and bring me home transformed by your presence. Amen.

Walk through the Sea

Scripture: "The LORD drove the sea back by a strong east wind all night, and turned the sea into dry land; and the waters were divided. The Israelites went into the sea on dry ground, the waters forming a wall for them on their right and on their left." (Exod 14:21b–22)

Reflection: An oxymoron is a phrase in which two words of contradictory meaning are used together for special effect. In the HB (OT) book of Exodus, the author of the narrative about Israel crossing the Sea of Reeds repeatedly uses the oxymoron of walking through the sea on dry ground (Exod 14:16, 21b, 22, 29; 15:19). Sea and dry ground are contradictory; they are meant to grab the reader's attention to make him or her pause and reflect on what is happening in the narrative. Experience informs us that walking into the sea results in getting wet, while walking on dry ground keeps us dry. But the author of this portion of Exodus declares that the Israelites walked into and through the sea and did not get wet; they remained dry. This account is designed to echo the first creation story, in which God orders the waters under the sky to be gathered together into one place so that dry land appears (Gen 1:9). God is not only creating a passageway through the sea, he is also creating a nation to be his own. As they walk on dry ground through the sea, they are passing through the birth canal which will enable them to enter the land God promised to Abraham, Isaac, and Jacob and leave Egypt, the deadly place of slavery, behind.

The journeys we take require us to leave the deadly place of order behind and for a time enter into oxymoronic chaos. God calls to us, like he did to Moses; he says to stretch out our walking sticks over the sea and divide it. We answer his call by walking through the sea on dry ground. We may need to divide ourselves from stress, abuse, joylessness, etc. and take the journey through the chaotic sea on dry ground to the other side, where we will be reborn, transformed, into the person God wants us to be. We may need to leave behind a job, house, or car, part sea water, and walk through to a new job, house, or car. While we walk through the sea, what is left behind drowns; it is covered by the water and dies. The Israelites, who had walked through the sea on dry ground, stood on the opposite shore and watched what had been for them transforming waters destroy the Egyptian chaos of their lives. Renewed as God's people, they continued their pilgrimage to the promised land.

Meditation/Journal: What sea have you recently walked through on dry land? What did you leave behind? How were you transformed?

Prayer: At your command, O LORD, the dry ground was revealed and the sea was swept away, when you delivered your people Israel from their enemy. As they walked through the sea on dry ground, you transformed them with your grace. Strengthen me with that same grace, and part the waters I encounter that I may walk through the seas on dry ground today, tomorrow, and forever. Amen.

Elijah and Elisha Walk Together

Scripture: "When they had crossed [the Jordan River], Elijah said to Elisha, 'Tell me what I may do for you, before I am taken from you.' Elisha said, 'Please let me inherit a double share of your spirit.' He responded, 'You have asked a hard thing; yet if you see me as I am being taken from you, it will be granted you; if not, it will not.' As they continued walking and talking, a chariot of fire and horses of fire separated the two of them, and Elijah ascended in a whirlwind into heaven." (2 Kgs 2:9–11)

Reflection: Sometimes we walk alone, and sometimes we walk with another. Elijah spent most of his life walking alone, and, after him, Elisha did the same. However, after crossing the Jordan River on dry ground (2 Kgs 2:8), they walk and talk until Elijah is transformed into heavenly glory. Elisha recrosses the river on dry ground, rejoins a company of prophets, and continues walking and talking on the journey of answering God's call. On their individual journey, both Elijah and Elisha spent much time in solitude leaving the order of their world and contemplating the word they were hearing from God. With lots of preparation, they answered the call and took the journey, momentarily walking with each other and with others, until they were transformed. Elijah was taken into heaven in a fiery chariot, and Elisha continued to raise people from the dead even after his body was placed in a tomb![1]

While it may not be a prophet with whom we walk, a companion on the journey can be of help to sort through the various aspects of walking. For some people, their spouse is their companion on the trip; for others it may be a best friend. Hikers often have designated companions with whom they have hiked before. Mountain climbers have designated companions whom they trust with their lives. While Elijah kept trying to separate himself from his companion three times, Elisha was determined to receive a double share of Elijah's spirit (2 Kgs 2:2, 4, 6, 9). And he does. That's what can happen when two people walk and talk together.

Meditation/Journal: Who has been a companion with you on your journey? In what specific ways did he or she help you hear God's call to take the journey? How were you transformed?

Prayer: God of Elijah and Elisha, you made your prophets companions on their journey to transformation. Send me a companion filled with your Holy Spirit. Grant that the grace we share may mutually strengthen our desire to keep walking and talking as you transform us through each other. Amen.

Satan's Walk

Scripture: "One day the heavenly beings came to present themselves before the LORD, and Satan also came among them. The LORD said to Satan, 'Where have you come from?' Satan answered the LORD, 'From going to and fro on the earth, and from walking up and down on it.'" (Job 1:6–7; 2:2)

Reflection: The HB (OT) book of Job begins with a scene taking place in God's heavenly court. Because the Holy One is presumed to be a king, like any other king he has a retinue, which consists of himself, officials, servants, and guests. The royal court takes place in a magnificent room dominated by the king's throne. According to the book of Job, one member

---

1. For more on Elijah and Elisha, see *From Contemplation to Action: The Spiritual Process of Divine Discernment Using Elijah and Elisha as Models* by Mark G. Boyer (Eugene, OR: Wipf and Stock, 2018).

of God's court is Satan. On a certain day, according to the narrator of the story about Job, the heavenly beings—the sons of God—come and present themselves before the LORD along with the Satan. In other words, God holds court in order to conduct heavenly business. Satan is not any kind of evil spirit, which ultimately develops into a demon or the devil. He is the accuser, a type of heavenly officer or prosecutor, whose function is to question and to test the genuineness of human virtue. Satan tests the reaction of people to sickness, natural catastrophes, etc. Virtue is not genuine unless it sustains such adversity. Thus, God recommends the virtue of Job, who is described as blameless, upright, and fearing God. While walking on the earth, Satan has witnessed the blessings Job has received; being true to his adversarial function, Satan is given permission to test Job, and he does. Job remains virtuous even in the face of the destruction of his family and property. In the second scene, the heavenly court convenes again, and again God recommends Job. The Adversary requests and is given permission to afflict Job's body with sores as a test of his blamelessness and uprightness. This scene launches the appearance of Job's friends, who, along with Job, try to decipher why such suffering has befallen Job, who knows nothing about Satan's and God's wager in heaven!

While we no longer presume that there is a heavenly court with God and Satan among the members, we still walk the earth to and fro and up and down pondering things that happen to us during our journey. Adversaries, who test genuineness, blamelessness, and uprightness are abundant. The driver who cuts into traffic is a test of our patience. The clerk who hands us a twenty-dollar bill instead of a ten-dollar bill tests our blamelessness. Our uprightness is tested by the truth we tell or the truth we hide. In the book of Job, Satan is the adversary who tests; in the book of our lives, the adversary remains; he merely has a different name! In order to maintain our genuineness, social order may need to be abandoned, because we hear a different call, like Job, and answer it by taking the journey and being transformed. Job's journey is recorded in the forty-two chapters of the book that bears his name and records his travels with God and the adversaries he encountered all along the way. Our book is recorded in our memories of walking in the Divine Presence genuinely, blamelessly, and uprightly.

Meditation/Journey: What adversaries have you encountered on your journey? How did each transform you?

Prayer: Naked I came from my mother's womb, O LORD, and naked shall I return there. You give, and you take way. No purpose of yours can be thwarted. Blessed be your name, O LORD, now and forever. Amen.

Walking through the Darkness

Scripture: "Even though I walk through the darkest valley, I fear no evil; for you [, LORD,] are with me; your rod and your staff—they give comfort to me." (Ps 23:4)

Reflection: According to biblical authors, there are many types of darkness to walk through on a journey. After declaring the LORD to be his shepherd, the psalmist declares that he does not fear anything because the LORD walks with him, relying on his shepherd's crook for protection and comfort. In Psalms 42 and 43, the authors ask God: "Why must I walk about mournfully because the enemy oppresses me?" (Pss 42:9b; 43:2b) In his songs, he states that hope in God will sustain him through the darkness. In Psalm 82, the singer petitions God, who is holding court, to give justice to the weak, the orphan, and the needy, who "walk around in darkness" (Ps 82:5a), by delivering them from the wicked. Isaiah states that justice is far away and righteousness does not reach him; "we wait for light, and lo! there is darkness; and for brightness, but we walk in gloom" (Isa 59:9). After coming to the conclusion "that wisdom excels folly as light excels darkness" (Eccl 2:13), the author of the HB (OT) book of Ecclesiastes declares, "The wise have eyes in their head, but fools walk in darkness" (Eccl 2:14). The prophet Isaiah makes clear that God's servants often walk in darkness and have no light, but they trust in the name of the LORD and rely upon their God (Isa 50:10).

Darkness seems to be always in the process of extinguishing the light. Leaving the previous order of the world is a walk out of the light and into the darkness. Hearing God's call and getting ready to answer it is a walk out of the light of knowing and into the darkness of unknowing. The path of the journey is filled with darkness creeping in on the light. Coming home from the journey—no matter what it may have been—is an act of walking out of the light of transformation and into the darkness again. The interplay of darkness—fear, mourning, oppression, injustice—and light—confidence, cheer, freedom, justice—surround the journey.

Meditation/Journal: On your most recent journey experience, what darkness did you encounter? What light disclosed God walking with you?

Prayer: You are my shepherd, O LORD, and I do not want. Lead me in right paths, and, when I walk through dark valleys, let me know your presence that comforts me. Grant that I may receive your goodness and mercy all the days of my life and dwell in your house forever. Amen.

Walk about Zion

Scripture: "Walk about Zion, go all around it, count its towers, consider well its ramparts; go through its citadels, that you may tell the next generation that this is God, our God forever and ever. He will be our guide forever." (Ps 48:12–14)

Reflection: The psalmist describes a walk on the walls around Jerusalem. While we no longer live in walled cities, there are still a few of them on the planet. One may think of the Great Wall of China, Hadrian's Wall in England, the walled city of York in England, the walled city of Avignon, France, the walled city of Avila, Spain, or the walled compound of the Kremlin in Moscow, Russia. In the U.S., we call them forts! The psalmist points out some of the distinguishing features of the walled city of Jerusalem built on Mount Zion. The walker should journey all around the wall, counting its towers, tall buildings characteristic of fortresses. The walker is exhorted to consider well its ramparts, fortified embankments, upon which the wall is constructed. The psalmist sings about going through the citadels, fortified buildings in the city used as places of refuge. Just as the wall protects Jerusalem and those who walk into the house of God (Ps 55:14) and into the glory of God (Bar 5:7), so does God protect people, especially those who walk humbly with him (Mic 6:8), a point to be made by one generation to the next. In other words, the power seen in the walls of the city reveal the power of the God who lives within them.

Since most of us cannot walk around a city wall in admiration, like the psalmist could do, we can see the power of God today in the buildings that dot our city landscapes. We can walk around economically mighty skyscrapers and let them proclaim the power of God. Places of worship—churches, synagogues, mosques, etc.—can be circumnavigated and observed to witness the power of the God worshipped within them. Even walking around one's home and paying attention to its style of construction, the materials used to build it, and its placement on a plot of land may reveal the God in whom the inhabitants believe. The psalmist reveals an aspect of the journey, namely, paying attention to what surrounds us while walking about, around, through, or on it. Seeing or touring a city wall or a building on the journey may spark transformation within us.

Meditation/Journal: What building has most recently caught your attention? What did it say to you? What did it say about God to you? What transformation did it spark in you?

Prayer: Great are you, O LORD, and greatly are you praised in all types of buildings around the world. You have been my defense, and I ponder your steadfast love. May my proclamation of your name reach to the ends of the earth forever and ever. Amen.

Walk through Fire

Scripture: " . . . [T]hus says the LORD . . . : . . . [W]hen you walk through fire you shall not be burned, and the flame shall not consume you." (Isa 43:1a, 2c)

Reflection: The HB (OT) book of Proverbs poses two questions to the reader: "Can fire be carried in the bosom without burning one's clothes? Or can one walk on hot coals without scorching the feet?" (Prov 6:27–28) Of course, both questions have to be answered "No." Any kind of fire held close to the breast will set one's clothes afire. Likewise, unless one is a trained firewalker, placing one's feet on hot coals will result in burns. Nevertheless, true to his promise in the prophet Isaiah, the LORD protects Shadrach (Hananiah), Meshach (Mishael), and Abednego (Azariah) after King Nebuchadnezzar throws them into a furnace of blazing fire. It doesn't take the king long to see "four men unbound, walking in the middle of the fire, and they are not hurt; and the fourth has the appearance of a god" (Dan 3:25). The king orders them to come out of the fire; "the hair on their heads was not singed, their tunics were not harmed, and not even the smell of fire came from them" (Dan 3:27). The king declares that their God has sent an angel to deliver his servants who walked through the fire while trusting in him. In the OT (A) Prayer of Azariah and the Song of the Three Jews, the narrator declares, "They walked around in the midst of the flames, singing hymns to God and blessing the Lord" (Sg Three 1:1 [Dan 3:24]).

Walking through fire is not meant to be taken literally, unless one is properly dressed for it, like a firefighter! In the HB (OT), one aspect of a theophany, a manifestation of God's presence, is fire.[2] Thus, walking through fire while on a journey means that the LORD protects the pilgrim, just like he protected the three men tossed into the fiery furnace. Walking through fire is like getting a customer service representative on the phone to solve a problem not listed on the company's web pages. Straightening out identity theft is a walk through fire almost as frightening as getting the bank to correct a posting error. And when it comes to a crisis of faith, navigating the rising water is like walking through fire. But no matter what the troubles of daily life may be, God journeys with us to protect us.

Meditation/Journal: What recent fire have you walked through on your journey? How was God present to help and to protect you?

Prayer: O LORD, my God, my Savior, when I walk through fire, let me not be burned or consumed by the flames. Call me by name that I may be aware of your presence that redeems and protects me now and forever. Amen.

Fools Walk on the Road

Scripture: "The heart of the wise inclines to the right, but the heart of a fool to the left. Even when fools walk on the road, they lack sense, and show to everyone that they are fools." (Eccl 10:2–3)

Reflection: While we may not agree with the philosophy presented by the Teacher in the HB (OT) book of Ecclesiastes about the wise tending to walk on the road to the right and the fool to the left, we may, nevertheless, ponder the truth contained in the two verses. In the ancient world, the right was the side of power, and the left was the side of weakness. Thus, the Teacher declares that wisdom imparts power to those who possess it, while foolishness leaves one powerless. The unintelligent or thoughtless person, who lacks good sense or judgment, displays his or her ridiculousness when walking on the road and using no common sense. In other words, the fool rejects wisdom's understanding and embraces its lack, thinking every person is

---

2. For more on the significance of fire, see *Divine Presence: Elements of Biblical Theophanies* by Mark G. Boyer (Eugene, OR: Wipf and Stock, 2017) 64–73.

a fool. The wise person possesses a good understanding and is guided by it, while the fool goes off in a bad and wrong way. A few verses later, the author confirms his wisdom by writing: "I have seen slaves on horseback, and princes walking on foot like slaves" (Eccl 10:7). In other words, slaves can be wise, and princes can be fools; slavery does not make one a fool, just as royalty does not make one wise.

Wisdom is acquired by reflecting on one's experiences of life on the journey, while also listening to the reflections of one's elders. According to the prophet Isaiah, God, the LORD, " . . . gives breath to the people upon [the earth] and spirit to those who walk in it" (Isa 42:5c). Using those gifts, those on a journey are inspired to listen intently and reflect upon the need to leave something old behind in order to prepare for the next phase of the journey. Taking the trip requires even more reflection on what is discovered. Through contemplation, a person is transformed gradually over and over, until he or she comes home to realize that much change has occurred in his or her life. Reflecting on the dialogue with one's best friend, on the time spent walking through the garden and what was observed there, and even on the encounter with one's dog results in a heart filled with wisdom. Letting such experiences escape without assigning meaning to them results in a heart filled with foolishness. Wisdom is spiritual power; foolishness is spiritual powerlessness.

Meditation/Journal: Over the past three days what wisdom did you gain by reflecting on your experiences? What experiences not reflected upon left you in foolishness?

Prayer: O LORD, before all else you created Wisdom. Then, you gave breath to the people upon your earth and spirit to those who walk on it. As I reflect upon the experiences of my journey, fill me with your wisdom from on high that I may be transformed over and over again forever. Amen.

Walking by Water

Scripture: " . . . [T]hus says the LORD: I will let [my people] walk by brooks of water, in a straight path in which they shall not stumble; for I have become a father to Israel, and Ephraim is my firstborn." (Jer 31:7a, 9bc)

Reflection: The Bible is filled with words for water, like river, stream, brook, etc. When writing about the return of the Jews to Jerusalem after their exile in Babylon, the prophet Jeremiah echoes words describing the exodus from Egypt. Seeing the people's return as a new exodus, Jeremiah portrays God declaring that his people would walk by brooks of water; water represents life in the "good land, a land with flowing streams, with springs and underground waters welling up in valleys and hills," states Moses (Deut 8:7). There, in the promised land, people could eat their fill and bless the LORD their God for the good land that he gave them (Deut 8:10), a land with flowing streams (Deut 10:7). The psalmist refers to the returnees as the redeemed, whom the LORD led "by a straight way" (Ps 107:7), which is also echoed by Jeremiah. There is a calming effect of a walk by water. Psalm 23 emphasizes that when its author states that the LORD leads him beside still waters (Ps 23:2b). In the CB (NT), Jesus not only leads his disciples beside still waters, but he stills the waters (Mark 1:16; Matt 4:18; Luke 5:1) and walks on the sea (Mark 6:47–51b; Matt 14:22–33; John 6:16–21).

Some journeys or parts of journeys require that we walk by brooks of water. The trail may not be all that straight, especially if it follows the path of the river, creek, or stream. The calming effect of walking along a waterway—even on an ocean's shore or around a pond or lake—is an act of leaving our ordered world behind. In the sound of the babbling, murmuring, roaring, or whispering brook, we can hear the voice of God calling us to prepare for another journey. The walk by water is a journey itself which is transforming us while we travel the straight path set before us. We may be changed from anger to humor, from grief to joy, from frustration to satisfaction, etc., because we walked by the water. Just like the exodus— which began when the attendants of pharaoh's daughter walked beside the Nile River (Exod 2:5)—and the new exodus were transforming events for the Jews, so our walk by water can change us.

Meditation/Journal: What effect did your most recent walk by water have on you? How was it transformative?

Prayer: In your great wisdom, O God, you led your people on paths by waterways that brought them life on their journey and more life in the promised land. As I walk by streams, creeks, and brooks or along oceans, lakes, and ponds transform me with new life today, tomorrow, and forever. Amen.

WALK

Walk on the Roof

Scripture: "It happened, late one afternoon, when [King] David rose from his couch and was walking about on the roof of the king's house, that he saw from the roof a woman bathing; the woman was very beautiful." (2 Sam 11:2)

Reflection: Contrary to modern practice, ancient people often spent time on the roof of their home. The above verse from the Second Book of Samuel presents King David awakening from a nap on the roof of the king's house in Jerusalem and walking around the roof to look over the city around his house. There he spots a woman—Bathsheba—bathing, another activity that could take place on the roof. The prophet Daniel notes that King Nebuchadnezzar of Babylon walked on the roof of his royal palace (Dan 4:29). The roof was used as a place to dry stalks of flax and to hide spies (Josh 2:6), to cool off (Judg 3:20–25), to sleep (1 Sam 9:25–26), to pitch a tent (2 Sam 16:22; Jdt 8:5), to build a room for the prophet Elisha (2 Kgs 4:10), to build booths (Neh 8:16), to make offerings to gods (Jer 19:13; 32:29; Zeph 1:5), and a place to pray (Acts 10:9). The roof of a house had to be somewhat flat for such activities to occur.

Comparable to walking on the roof biblically is having an upper deck or a porch built over a garage or other second-floor room accessible only from inside the house. Multi-level apartments and skyscrapers often have an accessible roof, where plants are grown, parties are held, and people can gaze over the area in which they live. While walking on the roof, one must put into perspective what he or she sees. This is what King David did not do; he saw only a naked woman, whom he summoned to his chamber and with whom he slept. Those on a journey who have left the previous order behind after hearing the call and preparing to travel often need to check the perspective during the trip. Without a clear picture of the destination, it is easy to get lost. David got lost because his focus was too narrow, too nearsighted, with little transformation. He needed to be farsighted, which would have enhanced his transformation and kept him away from the woman taking a bath on her roof, while he walked on his roof.

Meditation/Journal: While standing on the roof, deck, or upper porch of your home, what do you see? What is near you? What is far from you? What transformation comes about from each?

Prayer: LORD God, you provide clear vision to those who stop to consider the direction of their journey. Fill me with your Holy Spirit that my destination may be ever before me. Bring me home transformed. Amen.

How to Walk

Scripture: "When you walk, [your father's commandment and your mother's teaching] will lead you . . . ." (Prov 6:22a)

Reflection: We learn to walk as a child by beginning to crawl, then standing while holding onto something, then letting go and taking a step or two before falling. After getting our balance under control, we begin walking. Most children begin walking when they are about one year old. The author of the HB (OT) book of Proverbs declares that on the spiritual walk, our father's rules and our mother's instruction lead us. The prophet Hosea states that Israel is a child, whom God taught to walk (Hos 11:3a). Isaiah emphasizes that the LORD seems to have to teach walking over and over again: " . . . [T]hose who wait for the LORD shall renew their strength, they shall mount up with wings like eagles, they shall run and not be weary, they shall walk and not faint" (Isa 40:31). The OT (A) book of Sirach proposes that a person shows who he or she is through dress, laughter, "and the way he [or she] walks" (Sir 19:30). The author of Sirach notes that Aaron, brother of Moses and the first priest of Israel, wore bells as part of his clothes so that he sent "forth a sound as he walked" (Sir 45:9b). Thus, a journey is learning again how to walk.

Leaving behind the way we once ordered our world—daily schedule, daily work, daily meals, daily play, daily prayer—is a response to hearing God's call. We wait for God, listening intently for a word. Once it is heard, we prepare ourselves—take inventory, create an itinerary, pack—for the journey. All of this is like learning to walk again. God is the teacher, who leads us with his call. Every time we hear the call and answer it, we learn to walk again. We are renewed through the journey; we come home transformed. Our way of walking reveals that we are children of a loving God; the sound of our footsteps on the earth enables us and others to hear our walking.

Meditation/Journal: Which of your father's rules accompanies you on your journey? Which of your mother's teachings accompanies you on your journey? How many times have you learned to walk?

Prayer: When I was a child, O God, you loved me and called me to walk with you. You took me in your arms and wrapped me in bands of kindness and love, often lifting me to your cheek. Teach me again how to walk and give me the strength not to grow weary or to faint as I continue my journey in answer to your call. Amen.

A Day's Walk

Scripture: " . . . Jonah set out and went to Nineveh, according to the word of the LORD. Now Nineveh was an exceedingly large city, a three days' walk across. Jonah began to go into the city, going a day's walk. And he cried out, 'Forty days more, and Nineveh shall be overthrown!' And the people of Nineveh believed God; they proclaimed a fast, and everyone, great and small, put on sackcloth." (Jonah 3:3–5)

Reflection: The HB (OT) book of Jonah is a four-chapter story about a prophet, who tries not to respond to the call that he hears from the LORD. God tells Jonah to go to Nineveh, the capital of Assyria, feared and hated by the Israelites, but the prophet decides to escape by boarding a ship going the opposite direction! Of course, the LORD sees to it that he is thrown overboard, swallowed by a large fish and remaining for three days in the belly of the fish, and deposited on dry land, where he heard the word of the LORD again. This time he left the old order of things behind; an Israelite prophet is sent to his Assyrian enemy to preach repentance! Jonah answered the call and prepared himself. Nineveh was a huge metropolis which took a three days' journey—signifying the divine presence—to traverse. However, all Jonah needed was one day's walk preaching throughout the city. To his sheer wonderment, Jonah discovered that the people believed God, fasted, put on sackcloth, and repented. Thus, not only did God change his mind about what he had intended to do to Nineveh, but Jonah was transformed to see that all people, even his enemies, are God's people, upon whom he bestows grace, mercy, and love (Jonah 4:2). All this took place with one day's walk.

Similar transformation, albeit not quite as dramatic as Jonah's, is displayed in Luke's CB (NT) unique account of two travelers on the road to Emmaus three days after Jesus' death (Luke 24:13–35). They are on their way out of Jerusalem, when the risen Christ joins them as a fellow disguised journeyer. In dialogue they explain what happened to Jesus of Nazareth and how their hopes were crushed for a new order of living. Disguised Jesus reminds them of what their HB (OT) teaches about suffering preceding glory. Then, he joins them in a motel for the evening, breaks bread with them, and disappears as quickly as he had appeared. Their burning hearts remind them of their call, which they answer by making a return journey to Jerusalem, where they not only recount the transformation they have received, but listen as others do the same. Again, all this took place on a day's walk. A day's walk can be a morning or afternoon hike through a park or conservation area, a day spent at home in silence and solitude, a visit to the graves of family members in a cemetery, or a stop to pray in or around churches, temples, synagogues, etc. in the area where one lives. Sometimes all it takes is a day's walk.

Meditation/Journal: When have you experienced a call from God to leave the old order behind, prepared to answer the call, took the one-day walk, and returned home transformed?

Prayer: After but one day's walk through Nineveh, you, gracious God, transformed people's hearts through the preaching of Jonah. Out of your merciful and steadfast love make me aware of your transforming presence in every step I take this day. Amen.

Walk in Paths

Scripture: In days to come, "Many peoples shall come and say, 'Come, let us go up to the mountain of the LORD, to the house of the God of Jacob; that he may teach us his ways and that we may walk in his paths.'" (Isa 2:3)

Reflection: There are two ways to understand the word *path* in the passage from the prophet Isaiah. The prophet may be writing about a physical path, a track over which one walks from one place to another. He also may be writing about a metaphorical path, ethical themes, the conduct of God and humanity, and the character of God's salvation. Isaiah's contemporary, the prophet Micah, also presents the same words about many nations streaming to Jerusalem's Temple to be taught God's ways by the LORD so that they can walk in his paths (Mic 4:2). The author of the HB (OT) book of Proverbs exhorts his reader to keep sound wisdom and prudence so that he or she "will walk on [the] way securely and [his or her] foot will not stumble" (Prov 3:23). The OT (A) book of 2 Esdras presents Ezra reflecting on walking the path by narrating a parable about a city built on a plain that is full of all good things. However, there is only one path wide enough for one person to walk on to enter the city, and there is fire on the right and deep water on the left. According to the prophet Ezra, only the living who pass through the difficult experiences (fire and water) of life (path) can ever enter the city reserved for them (2 Esd 7:6–15).

If walking in ancient paths does not resonate with the reader, then following the sidewalks (paths) of city streets might. Describing the fall of Jerusalem to the Babylonians in 587 BCE, the author of the HB (OT) book of Lamentations states that the Babylonian army "dogged" the people's "steps so that [they] could not walk in [their] streets" (Lam 4:18), while the prophet Zephaniah describes how the streets had been laid waste so that no one walked on them (Zeph 3:6b). Taking a walk in a path (street)—physical or ethical—is the act of leaving the order of one's home or business behind to think about life. God's call may be heard, and one has to prepare to walk the path or along the street through fire on one side and water on the other side. The journey is always dangerous, but the return brings one home transformed.

Meditation/Journal: What recent walk in a path or along a street brought you home transformed? What fire and water did you think about while you walked?

Prayer: I walk the paths of my life in faithfulness to you, O LORD. Continue to teach me to walk in your truth and give me an undivided heart to revere your name. Grant me the grace to walk before you in the land of the living and be transformed to walk before you in the life of the world to come. Amen.

Idols Cannot Walk

Scripture: "... [I]dols are silver and gold, the work of human hands. They have ... feet, but do not walk.... Those who make them are like them; so are all who trust in them." (Ps 115:4, 7–8)

Reflection: Among the many characteristics of idols—statues or carved images worshiped as gods—presented by the psalmists is that they have feet, but they cannot walk. The psalmists declare idols worthless (Pss 31:6; 97:7). According to Psalm 96, "all the gods of the peoples are idols" (Ps 96:5). "The idols of the nations are silver and gold, the work of human hands," according to Psalm 135:15. "Those who make them and all who trust them shall become like them" (Ps 135:18). While idols are rendered powerless, even to walk, the issue addressed by the psalmists is trust in the LORD, who walks (Gen 3:8) and who helps and protects his people, who walk. The prophet Jeremiah relays the LORD's words to Israel about not learning the ways of the nations because their idols have to be carried; they cannot walk (Jer 10:5b). The author of the OT (A) book of Wisdom is harsher, writing that Israel's enemies "thought that all their heathen idols were gods, ... and their feet [were] of no use for walking" (Wis 15:15). Likewise, the CB (NT) book of Revelation states that those who continue to worship the work of their hands—idols of gold and silver and bronze and stone and wood which cannot walk—have not repented (Rev 9:20–21).

The psalmist states that all who make idols and trust them are like them, that is, powerless. The pilgrim wants to keep that truth in mind while on the lifetime journey. It is easy to unconsciously worship a non-walking idol. A home itself or the wide-screen TV housed within it easily can become a non-walking idol, especially on Superbowl Sunday. A luxury car with lots of bells and whistles is a non-walking—although rolling—idol for some people. Another non-ambulatory idol is money; while it cannot walk on its own, it is carried by almost everyone. Even people can become walking idols, such as movie stars, band members, and talk show hosts or hostesses. Because of the readily availability of non-waking idols, the process for the journeyer is of utmost importance. The world of the idol needs to be left behind after hearing the divine call and making preparation. Taking the journey reveals the non-walking idols in our lives. Then, we come home transformed, consciously aware of the silver and gold, the work of our hands, that became non-walking idols.

Meditation/Journal: What non-walking idol have you become aware of most recently? What was your response to your awareness? What transformation took place within you?

Prayer: Not to me, O LORD, not to me, but to your name give glory, for the sake of your steadfast love and faithfulness. Grace me with great trust, you who are my help and protector. Bless me, as I give you praise now and forever. Amen.

Walking Bowed

Scripture: " . . . [T]he person who is deeply grieved, who walks bowed and feeble, with failing eyes and famished soul, will declare your glory and righteousness, O Lord." (Bar 2:18)

Reflection: One who walks bowed and feeble shows appropriate respect and deference while grieving, while being specifically lost in meditation, or while caught up in praise of God. The prophet Baruch writes about those who are processing grief walking bowed; his audience seems to be the elderly, who are feeble with failing eyesight and hungry for spiritual uplifting. The author of the OT (A) book of Sirach cautions his readers about one "who walks bowed down" who may be an enemy (Sir 12:11), while the author of the HB (OT) book of Exodus legislates that a person who has been injured with a stone or a fist in a dispute and recovers, having to walk "around outside with the help of a staff" (Exod 21:19), is liable for the loss of time during recovery. Those who possess wisdom and walk the paths of uprightness walk with unhampered steps and run without stumbling, according to Proverbs (4:12). Walking with bowed head, even while using a staff for support, is appropriate at some times in a person's life.

Walking or hiking with a bowed head through a large garden, park, or conservation area and getting caught up with the beauty of blooming and variously-shaded green plants at one's feet can lead to praise of the Creator. Walking with bowed head through a cemetery to the grave of a loved one not only brings memories to mind, but reminds us that we mourn the passing of some people our whole life long. While traversing a path in the country or a sidewalk in the city, we may bow our head to sort through a problem; intense thinking causes many people to lower their head so as not to be distracted in deep thought. All of these and other walks with bowed head are examples of leaving an ordered world behind in order to respond to a call to take a journey. All bring us home transformed to one degree or another, while declaring the glory and righteousness of God.

Meditation/Journal: When have you most recently journeyed with your head bowed? What was the occasion for the walk? What transformation occurred in you?

Prayer: LORD God, with bowed head I walk in your presence seeking your righteousness like the glory of the light of dawn, which shines brighter and brighter until the day is full of light. Direct my steps away from darkness so that I do not stumble. Keep me attentive to your words all the days of my life. Amen.

Walk in a Field

Scripture: The sovereign Lord said to Ezra: "'. . .[Y]ou have devoted your life to wisdom, and called understanding your mother. Therefore I have shown you these things; for there is a reward laid up with the Most High. For it will be that after three more days I will tell you other things, and explain weighty and wondrous matters to you.' Then I got up and walked in the field, giving great glory and praise to the Most High for the wonders that he does from time to time, and because he governs the times and whatever things come to pass in their seasons. And I stayed there three days." (2 Esd 13:55–58)

Reflection: After the Most High has shown Ezra what happened to the ten lost tribes of Israel conquered and dispersed by the Assyrian King Shalmaneser in 722 BCE, he praises the prophet for having devoted his life to wisdom and understanding God's ways. As the Almighty makes clear, he is not yet finished calling Ezra to leave the order of his world, because he is wise enough to hear the call and prepare himself to answer it. God will show him more on the journey of revelation. And each vision will leave him transformed over and over again. However, there is more going on in the passage from Second Esdras, signified by three days. Three is the number signifying divine presence.[3] There is no doubt that Ezra has been having mystical experiences, and he is being promised more of them. To ground

---

3. For more on the significance of sacred numbers, see *Divine Presence: Elements of biblical Theophanies* by Mark G. Boyer (Eugene, OR: Wipe and Stock, 2017) 10-25.

himself, he takes a walk in a field giving glory and praise to God for his works and his providence concerning times and seasons. The last vision that he will receive after three days makes his days of solitude and fasting forty. Thus, he is like Moses, who fasted forty days and nights on Mount Horeb (Sinai) (Exod 34:28), and like the prophet Elijah, who, after receiving bread and water from the angel of the LORD, walked forty days and nights to the same mountain (1 Kgs 19:8). Both Moses and Elijah enjoyed mystical experiences on Mount Horeb (Sinai).

Like Ezra, we do not need to climb a mountain to be transformed; a walk in a field will do. Some parts of the country make walking in a wheat, corn, rice, or soybean field easy to do. While watching the wind sway and ripple the crop, one may experience the divine presence. For those who live within cities, a walk in a garden, park, or backyard may lift one's awareness to marvel at the work of God from one season to another—which is an experience of the divine. Walking a city or town trail upon which we meet other walkers, hikers, and bikers can create a sense of community with others, and that experience is nothing other than the divine presence with us on our journey. Walking in a field of any kind leaves us transformed and ready for the next vision that changes us again.

Meditation/Journal: In what field have you recently walked? What moved you to give glory and praise to God? What transformation did you experience?

Prayer: Most High, from one season to the next you have revealed yourself to me on my walks in a field. You have deemed me worthy to have my prayer heard by you. Graciously keep me aware of your divine presence, and I will give you glory and praise today, tomorrow, and forever. Amen.

Stand Up and Walk

Scripture: "When Jesus perceived [the scribes' and Pharisees'] questionings, he answered them, 'Why do you raise such questions in your hearts? Which is easier to say, "Your sins are forgiven you," or to say, "Stand up and walk?" But so that you may know that the Son of Man has authority on earth to forgive sins'—he said to the one who was paralyzed—'I say to you, stand up and take your bed and go to your home.' Immediately he stood up before them, took what he had been lying on, and went to his home, glorifying God." (Luke 5:22–25)

Reflection: The account of the paralyzed man being taken to Jesus and lowered through the thatched roof originates in Mark's Gospel (2:3–12). The author of Matthew's Gospel eliminates the roof scene (Matt 9:2–8), but the author of Luke's Gospel presents the man lowered through the roof tiles (Luke 5:18–26). Both Matthew and Luke alter Mark's story to fit their own themes and audiences. Some of the background to the account may come from the LORD's words in the HB (OT) book of Leviticus: " . . . I have broken the bars of your yoke and made you walk erect" (Lev 26:13b). Likewise, Isaiah declares that "the lame shall leap like a deer" (Isa 35:6a) when the Jews return to Jerusalem. Because Luke, in the Acts of the Apostles, likes to portray Peter and Paul doing what Jesus did in the gospel, Peter addresses a man lame from birth with the words " . . . [S]tand up and walk" (Acts 3:6), and Paul addresses a man who had never walked with the words "Stand upright on your feet" (Acts 14:10). In both instances, the men begin to walk.

While not questioning the miraculous nature of the biblical accounts of healing the handicapped, we need to apply the story to those on a journey today. Hearing the call to stand up and walk implies leaving one's previous handicapped world behind in order to take a journey. There are physical handicaps, and there are mental handicaps that need to be considered. The physically handicapped may need the assistance of crutches, a walker, a wheelchair, or an artificial limb, but that does not keep them from taking the journey. The mentally handicapped may be stuck in excuses as to why the journey cannot be made, fear of travel, or responsibilities that keep one at home. While all must be considered, hearing the call must not be set aside to be some future endeavor. It needs to be answered with preparation; it needs to be taken within the realm of possibilities that exist for each person. Transformation awaits those who respond by standing up and walking in whatever way possible.

Meditation/Journal: When have you heard the call to stand up and walk? With what handicap did you have to deal in order to take the journey? What transformation occurred as a result?

Prayer: O LORD God, you call all people to walk erect and to leap like deer once they hear your call to journey that leads to transformation. Grant me the grace to discern your words and prepare myself to be changed on my journey. All glory be yours now and forever. Amen.

Walk

Walking Along

Scripture: "As [Jesus] walked along, he saw a man blind from birth. His disciples asked him, 'Rabbi, who sinned, this man or his parents, that he was born blind?' Jesus answered, 'Neither this man nor his parents sinned; he was born blind so that God's works might be revealed in him.'" (John 9:1–3)

Reflection: To walk along means to move or travel on legs and feet proceeding at a moderate pace from one place to another. In the passage from John's Gospel above, Jesus just left the Temple area and is traveling to an unidentified place, when he sees a blind man. His followers ask him a critical question based on an ancient presupposition that blindness resulted because someone—parents or man—sinned. Jesus' critical answer declares that no one sinned; the man's blindness has a purpose: to reveal God's works—which is shortly discovered to be the restoration of the unnamed man's sight (John 9:6–7). In a similar vein, Tobit, in the OT (A) book that bears his name, was blinded by bird droppings that fell into his eyes while he slept in his courtyard (Tob 2:10). His son, Tobias, at the word of Azariah (Raphael in disguise), his traveling companion, restores his father's sight (Tob 11:4, 7–14). Throughout the novelette, all the characters, including Tobit, have been revealing God's works. Immediately, Tobit reveals God's work of restoring his sight by going to meet his new daughter-in-law, "walking along in full vigor and with no one leading him" (Tob 11:16b).

After teaching a crowd of people, the author of Mark's Gospel narrates, "As [Jesus] was walking along" (Mark 2:14; Matt 9:9), he saw Levi (Luke 5:27; Matthew in Matt 9:9), whom he called to leave his tax-collecting booth and follow him. The tax collector got up and walked along with him. Jesus' call is to leave tax collecting—the old order of the world—behind and respond to his summons to walk along with him. Levi (Matthew) answers by leaving his post in order to be prepared by Jesus' teaching. He has already begun the journey, which will grow into a ministry he cannot yet foresee. And that ministry will continue the process of transformation that he has already undergone by abandoning his former means and way of life. Walking along will reveal God's works through and in him. What was true for the blind man, Tobit, and Levi (Matthew) is also true for us; we never know what God may reveal through us as we walk along.

Meditation/Journal: Where have you been recently walking along when you heard a call to take a journey? What transformation occurred as a result of answering the call?

Prayer: Blessed are you, God, and blessed be your great name, and blessed be all your holy angels, who walk along with those whom you call. May your holy name be blessed throughout all the ages by those to whom you show mercy. Amen.

Walk in the Light

Scripture: Jesus said to his disciples: "Are there not twelve hours of daylight? Those who walk during the day do not stumble, because they see the light of this world. But those who walk at night stumble, because the light is not in them." (John 11:9–10)

Reflection: The only times there are twelve hours of daylight and twelve hours of darkness are at the two annual equinoxes around March 20 and September 23; an equinox is the moment when the center of the sun is directly above earth's equator. While it is highly unlikely that Jesus asks his disciples the question about twelve hours of daylight exactly on an equinox, it is the point that he is making that counts. Earlier, he had explained: "I am the light of the world. Whoever follows me will never walk in darkness but will have the light of life" (John 8:12). And, Jesus had also said: "We must work the works of him who sent me while it is day; night is coming when no one can work. As long as I am in the world, I am the light of the world" (John 9:4–5). He told his disciples, "The light is with you for a little longer. Walk while you have the light, so that the darkness may not overtake you. If you walk in the darkness, you do not know where you are going. While you have the light, believe in the light, so that you may become children of the light" (John 12:35–36).

Those on a journey are instructed by the Johannine Jesus to follow the divine light to eternal life. God (Jesus) works in the light until Jesus' departure through death (night) and resurrection (light). As long as he was in the world, he was the light of the world, just like the sun is the light of the world. His light let others see how to accomplish God's works. Jesus' call to disciples then and now exhorts us to leave the old order of life, the darkness, behind and to take the journey, to walk with Jesus as the light shining the way. As he makes clear, those who follow him will not stumble; they will be transformed by the very light they follow. They will be changed into light. "What has come into being in him was life, and the life was the light of all people," writes the Johannine author (John 1:3b-4). Those walking on a journey know that "[t]he light shines in the darkness, and the darkness [does] not overcome it" (John 1:5). The true light, which enlightens all journeyers already came into the world (John 1:9).

Meditation/Journal: Where have you encountered the light on your journey? What works of God did you do? Where have you found darkness?

Prayer: Almighty God, you are light, and in you there is no darkness. Shine the light of your Son, Jesus, on me throughout my journey that I may accomplish the work you call me to do. Through the enlightenment of the Holy Spirit, lead me to the eternal light that transforms me forever and ever. Amen.

Walk in the Country

Scripture: " . . . [Jesus] appeared in another form to two of them [who had been with him], as they were walking into the country. And they went back and told the rest, but they did not believe them." (Mark 16:12-13)

Reflection: A perusal of the end of Mark's Gospel demonstrates that it has three endings. The original at 16:8 presents the women fleeing from the empty tomb and saying nothing to anyone about Jesus' resurrection. The second ending, two more sentences added to 16:8, is a commissioning scene. And the third ending, 16:9-20, from which the passage above is taken, is a summary of other material and endings from Luke's Gospel, Matthew's Gospel, and the Acts. Only Luke narrates the account about two disciples on Easter Sunday going to a village in the country about seven miles from Jerusalem (Luke 24:13). While they walk along, they are discussing the events of the past few days. The risen Jesus appears to them, but they do not recognize him, even as he teaches them throughout their walk in the country. By the time they get near the village, the unrecognized stranger indicates that he is walking on, but they invite him to join them for dinner. When he breaks bread with them, they recognize him, but he vanishes. They are so overwhelmed with transformation that they turn around and walk through the country back to Jerusalem, where they find the other disciples and tell their story to them (Luke 24:13–35).

While walking in the country, we may discover a companion—literally meaning one who shares bread—joining us, or maybe we invite someone to join us for a walk in the country. What the Lukan narrative discloses is that the physical journey of walking in the country manifests the spiritual journey. Two disciples are walking away from Jerusalem, where they had placed their dashed hopes. They need a companion to give them a new perspective, a new interpretation of their experiences. That is what Jesus, the alias stranger, does for them. As he talks, he sets their hearts on fire with new meaning. They are so enlivened that they turn around, leaving the new order to which they had fled in order to return to what they had left behind! They have heard again the call. So, they walk through the country from the village to Jerusalem. And there they discover others who have been transformed from despair to hope. All this took place because a stranger joined them on the road walking in the country.

Meditation/Journal: When have you encountered a stranger on a country walk that presented a different perspective to you? How did you respond?

Prayer: I walk before you, O LORD, with companions who join me on the way. Fill us with your grace that sheds new light on our experiences, and make us ever more aware of your presence. Amen.

Walking on All Fours

Scripture: "The LORD spoke to Moses and Aaron, saying to them: 'All winged insects that walk upon all fours are detestable to you. But among the winged insects that walk on all fours you may eat those that have jointed legs above their feet, with which to leap on the ground. Of them you may eat: the locust . . . , the cricket . . . , and the grasshopper . . . . But all other winged insects that have four feet are detestable to you.'" (Lev 11:1, 20–23)

Reflection: The HB (OT) book of Leviticus is a collection of laws gathered over time and written in a single book. The passage above comes from the section making a distinction between clean and unclean foods. The reference is not to food being clean because it was washed nor to it being dirty because it was not washed. Cleanness and uncleanness means being free from any physical, moral, or ritual contamination. If one ate any other insect except the locust, the cricket, and the grasshopper, he or she was unclean. The 613 laws of Torah stipulated a boundary that was not to be crossed in the Israelite social system. While we may be amused by the passage about which insects walking on four legs can be eaten and which cannot, the law was designed to preserve the holiness boundary within the community of God's people, who are holy because the LORD is present in their midst. Touching or eating winged insects that walked upon all fours—other than the locust, the cricket, and the grasshopper—left one unclean until the evening (Lev 11:24). Once the evening passed, one was clean again. Thus, for a short time a person placed himself or herself outside the holiness of the chosen community; once evening passed, he or she was readmitted.

While we have nothing that is similar to this Israelite law, we do have what we would consider to be socially acceptable table fare for a dinner party. In general, we would not serve roasted horse, barbecued dog, or fried snake. While back in the seventeenth century many people in what is now the rural U.S. ate racoon, opossum, and ground hog, very few would hunt or eat such creatures today. Even in the seventeenth century people did not eat skunk; it was beyond socially acceptable table fare! The point is that while on a journey there are foods that, depending upon the culture, are not appropriate to eat. Today some people may enjoy in-season, chocolate covered locusts, crickets, and grasshoppers. However, any other winged insects that have four feet—chocolate covered or not—should be avoided, according to Leviticus!

Meditation/Journal: What are the foods that you consider to be unholy to eat on your journey?

Prayer: To keep your people close to you, O LORD, you specified what foods separated them from your holy presence. Make me ever more grateful for the food I eat, and hear my thanksgiving for your many gifts. Draw me closer and closer in the circle of your holiness. Amen.

Don't Walk into a Pit

Scripture: Bildad the Shuhite said to Job: "[The wicked] are thrust into a net by their own feet, and they walk into a pitfall. A trap seizes them by the heel; a snare lays hold of them. A rope is hid for them in the ground, a trap for them in the path." (Job 18:8–10)

Reflection: In the HB (OT) book of Job, Bildad makes a response to Job by declaring him to be among the wicked. In the part of Bildad's speech quoted above, Bildad explains what happens to the wicked using hunting imagery. Using a variety of images, he has already told Job that the light of the wicked gets put out, that the flame of their fire does not shine, that the light is dark in their tent, and that their lamps are extinguished (Job 18:5-6). Then, Bildad describes a deep, disguised hole in the ground functioning as a trap, which is set to grab them by the heel and keep them underground. The hole is so deep that escape is impossible. According to Bildad, the pit is the place of those who do not know God (Job 18:21). Throughout the book, Job argues his righteousness; he is not among the wicked. In his response to Bildad, Job declares that God is hunting him (Job 19:6). Just like Bildad torments Job (19:2), in the prophet Isaiah, God declares that Jerusalem's enemies will assume his duty as tormentor of his people. The LORD says, " . . . I will put [the bowl of my wrath] into the hand of your tormentors, who have said to you, 'Bow down, that we may walk on you'; and you have made your back like the ground and like the street for them to walk on" (Isa 51:23).

Those on a journey should be wary of pits. After hearing a call and leaving the past behind in order to answer that summons, we take the journey, while paying attention to pitfalls. We want to avoid swindlers, those who obtain money by deception or fraud, either in public or on the telephone. Another pitfall is a legal entrapment found in the small print of a contract. Any kind of renting a room, a house, or a car can land a traveler into a pitfall. We don't want to be prey for tormentors, who try to walk all over us. At the same time, we also want to be conscious of those who may need authentic help. It is no easy task to sort wickedness from righteousness, but like Bildad and Job, it is a necessary task to keep from walking into a pit, while on a journey.

Meditation/Journal: When have you recently discovered yourself in a pitfall? How did you escape?

Prayer: I know that you, O LORD, my redeemer, live, and that you will rescue me from whatever pitfall I may experience on my journey. Preserve me from the traps of the wicked and guide my feet to you, whom I hope to behold one day in glory. Amen.

WALK

Walk in Procession

Scripture: " ... [T[hanks be to God, who in Christ always leads us in triumphal procession, and through us spreads in every place the fragrance that comes from knowing him. For we are the aroma of Christ to God among those who are being saved and among those who are perishing; to the one a fragrance from death to death, to the other a fragrance from life to life." (2 Cor 2:14–16a)

Reflection: A procession is a group of people walking forward in a line as part of a celebration, commemoration, or demonstration. In his Second Letter to the Corinthians, Paul uses the image of a victory march to explain the triumphal procession led by Christ. In Paul's world, a conquering general with his chief officers led his forces in procession through the city, while the air was filled with the aroma of burning incense, which signified life to the victors, but death to the conquered. The prophet Isaiah had written about the life of the victors in his description of the triumphal procession of the Jews returning from Babylonian captivity (Isa 60:1–22). The gates of Jerusalem would always remain open so that nations could bring their wealth, "with their kings led in procession" (Isa 60:11b). An account of the death of the conquered is found in the narrative of persecution of the Jews in the OT (A) Second Book of Maccabees; the author explains how the Jews—the conquered—were taken, under bitter constraint, to partake of Gentile sacrifices, "and when a festival of Dionysus was celebrated, they were compelled to wear wreaths of ivy and to walk in the procession in honor of Dionysus" (2 Macc 6:7).

One psalmist remembers how he "went with the throng, and led them in procession to the house of God, with glad shouts and songs of thanksgiving, a multitude keeping festival" (Ps 42:4). Another declares, "Your solemn processions are seen, O God, the processions of my God, my King, into the sanctuary—the singers in front, the musicians last, between them girls playing tambourines" (Ps 68:24–25). A public celebration of deliverance with a procession is described by the author of Psalm 118: "The LORD is God, and he has given us light. Bind the festal procession with branches, up to the horns of the altar" (Ps 118:27). While some of a journey is taken alone, parts of it may involve others, who have heard the call to leave their old lives behind after some preparation and walk in procession, while leaving the fragrance of Christ all along the way. That aroma, like burning incense, transforms others and all those walking in procession.

Meditation/Journal: When have you most recently walked in procession? Was it a celebration, a commemoration, or a demonstration? What aroma did it leave behind?

Prayer: I bless you, God, in the great processions that lead to more abundant life. Hear my prayer for the graces that produce endurance and insight. I offer this thanksgiving to you, O LORD, today, tomorrow, and forever. Amen.

Like Walking Trees

Scripture: "[Jesus] took the blind man by the hand and led him out of the village [of Bethsaida]; and when he had put saliva on his eyes and laid his hands on him, he asked him, 'Can you see anything?' And the man looked up and said, 'I can see people, but they look like trees, walking.' Then Jesus laid his hands on his eyes again; and he looked intently and his sight was restored, and he saw everything clearly." (Mark 8:23–25)

Reflection: The account of the blind man of Bethsaida is unique to Mark's Gospel. It is situated at the beginning of the journey narrative to signify to Markan readers that it takes time to understand that Jesus is a suffering Messiah, who will be put to death (Mark 8:31; 9:31; 10:33). The blind man, who once was able to see, comes to see again. However, he does not see things sharply and distinctly; he can barely tell the difference between humans and trees. After Jesus first puts saliva on his eyes and lays his hands on him, the blind man can only tell humans from trees by the fact that humans walk, but trees do not. It takes a second laying on of Jesus' hands on the blind man's eyes for him to see clearly. Jesus' method of using saliva and the laying on of hands to heal is echoed earlier in Mark's Gospel, when he heals a deaf man with a speech impediment in the same way (Mark 7:31–37). Also, in this account is a motif known as the Messianic secret: everyone in the story who should know who Jesus is never figures it out, while those who should not know who Jesus is do figure it out. That is why the once-blind man, who has been taken by Jesus out of the village, is told to go home and not enter the village (Mark 8:26), why the deaf man with the speech impediment is taken away from the crowd to be healed and told to tell no one (Mark 7:33, 36), and why at the end of the journey narrative, once-blind Bartimaeus follows Jesus on the way (Mark 10:52). The secret of the suffering Messiah is only gradually understood by those whose sight or hearing is restored.

The purpose of a journey is not always totally understood; its purpose is revealed gradually. Something deep within us urges us to some upsetting degree to leave behind the order of our world. We interpret the feeling as a call, and we begin to prepare to answer it. We, who were once full of sight, discover that we are now blind. We do not see things sharply and distinctly; we can barely tell the difference between humans and trees! However, the journey beckons us not to turn around, not to go into the village, but to follow Jesus through suffering and death to transformation. As we journey, we see only gradually. Sharpness increases. We can distinguish between people and trees! Discipleship is a gradual process during which things appear blurry, but with time and experience of travel they become clear.

Meditation/Journal: What recent journey began looking blurry and ended looking clearly? What important truth did you learn on the journey? How were you transformed?

Prayer: Lord Jesus Christ, lay your hands upon my eyes that I may see your way and follow you intently. Lay your hands upon my ears that I may hear your word that calls me to keep journeying to transformation in the kingdom, where you live and reign forever and ever. Amen.

6

Way

On the Way

Scripture: " . . . Saul said to the boy who was with him, 'Let us turn back, or my father will stop worrying about the donkeys [who strayed] and worry about us.' But he said to him, 'There is a man of God in this town; he is a man held in honor. Whatever he says always comes true. Let us go there now; perhaps he will tell us about the journey on which we have set out.' So they went to the town where the man of God was. As they were entering the town, they saw Samuel coming out toward them on his way up to the shrine." (1 Sam 9:5–6, 10b, 14b)

Reflection: In biblical literature, there are multiple uses for the phrase "on the way." In the passage above, Saul and an unnamed boy are searching for the donkeys belonging to Saul's father; the donkeys have strayed. The boy knows about Samuel, a seer and a prophet. The boy suggests that the two of them consult the man of God to find out where they might find the donkeys on their journey. As they climbed the hill upon which the town was built, they spy Samuel on the way to the shrine where sacrifices were offered. Samuel had already been informed by the LORD that he had chosen Saul to be the first king of Israel. Thus, once Saul and the boy catch up to Samuel, Samuel invites Saul to join him for the sacrifice and the feast that follows it. Then, after a good night's sleep, Samuel anoints Saul, pouring a vial of oil on his head and saying, "The LORD has anointed you ruler over his people Israel" (1 Sam 10:1a). Then, both Saul and Samuel continue on the way.

On the way can mean to keep moving, to keep traveling on the road. If for some reason the journey has been stalled, on the way means to pick up the trip where one stopped, to continue the journey. Getting from one place to another is to be on the way. Once we have heard the call, like Saul did to find the donkeys and Samuel to anoint Saul king of Israel, we leave behind the order of the past and prepare to take the journey. While on the way, there may be a side trip to visit a seer, a prophet, a holy person, a counselor, a confidant, etc. to get another opinion. The man who became king of Israel was urged by a boy to stop and consult Samuel. Taking time on the way to see Samuel resulted in Saul's transformation from donkey-seeker to king of Israel! While not losing focus, it doesn't hurt to stop on the way for a while to get information that can transform us for the next stage of the journey.

Meditation/Journal: When have you last stopped on the way to evaluate your journey and seek information for its continuance? What transformation did you experience as a result of the pause?

Prayer: Open my ears, O LORD, to listen to the inspired promptings of others, as I am on the way of my journey. Make me aware of your presence that guides me to you. I ask this in the name of your Son, Jesus, who is the way now and forever. Amen.

Guard the Way

Scripture: ". . . [T]he LORD God said, 'See, the man has become like one of us, knowing good and evil; and now, he might reach out his hand and take also from the tree of life, and eat, and live forever'—therefore the LORD God sent him forth from the garden of Eden, to till the ground from which he was taken. He drove out the man; and at the east of the garden of Eden he placed the cherubim, and a sword flaming and turning to guard the way to the tree of life." (Gen 3:22–24)

Reflection: The author of the HB (OT) book of Genesis employs the phrase *to guard the way* as a *Keep Out* sign. After the man and the woman eat of the tree of the knowledge of good and evil and God discovers what they have done and curses them for their misbehavior, he realizes that if they stay in the garden, they can eat of the tree of life and live forever. So, the LORD God decides that the couple must be expelled from the garden. To be sure that the man and the woman do not turn around and come back, God places a cherubim guard at the gate. To accompany the winged, half-human, half-beast creature, God installs a fiery, rotating sword, which blocks the way to the tree of life. The author of the HB (OT) book of Exodus records God telling Moses that he is "going to send an angel in front of [the Israelites], to guard [them] on the way and to bring [them] to the place that [he has] prepared" (Exod 23:20). This protecting being, who has God's name in him (Exod 23:21), is to be listened to attentively, and God will be an enemy to the Israelites' enemies and a foe to their foes (Exod 23:22). Thus, God will protect his people, he will guard the way to the promised land.

While we do not need to be concerned about passing the cherubim and revolving fiery sword guarding the gate into Eden, we may find consolation in the divine promise to guard us on our journey. Since the call to take the journey comes directly from God or indirectly through one of his prophets, we have assurance that we are being called from the security of our ordered world to prepare to leave it and take the journey into the unknown. While the Israelites had heard of the land promised to Abraham, Isaac, and Jacob, they did not know where it was until God led them to it through Moses and Joshua. Taking the journey from Egypt to it was an act of trust in the God who promised to guard them on the way. Not only would they arrive at the land transformed, but much more transformation awaited them, as they conquered the inhabitants of the territory that God promised them. The divine presence was with them, guarding their way.

Meditation/Journal: When have you most recently experienced God guarding your way? What transformation resulted from that experience?

Prayer: Ever-living God, send your angel to guard me on the way and bring me to the place you have prepared for me. As I journey, fill me with the grace of the Holy Spirit, who transforms me over and over again. Amen.

Holy Way

Scripture: "A highway shall be [in the wilderness], and it shall be called the Holy Way; . . . it shall be for God's people; no traveler, not even fools, shall go astray." (Isa 35:8).

Reflection: Isaiah paints a picture of hope for the Jews to return to Jerusalem and to rebuild Judah. The Holy Way will be like a highway through a wilderness that has burst into roadside gardens. The holy way highway is elevated above the surrounding earth, leveled, and cleared of large stones and any other obstructions. The remnant of God's freed-from-captivity people will follow this way of holiness to Jerusalem. In our own day and time, what Isaiah describes is like our Interstate Highways. All of them have a number to distinguish one from another, but sections of some have signs dedicating sections to patrols who died on them. All God's highways are holy ways. After discussing and bargaining with Abraham about the evil he found in Sodom, God went his holy way (Gen 18:33). Lot, Abraham's nephew, was about to learn quickly, "The way of the LORD is a stronghold for the upright, but destruction for evildoers" (Prov 10:29).

All journeys should be made on the holy way highway. We listen intently for the call to leave home and to prepare to do so. If we have listened and discerned carefully, we, like God's people before us, take the journey with the confidence that God will not let us go astray. That journey may be to a court room to support a friend. It may be to the local soup kitchen or pantry to feed the hungry. Our journey may be to join a protest march on the street to defend the life, dignity, and rights of others. Those and others are holy ways traveled by God's people. And those holy ways lead both to individual and group transformation for those who travel them.

Meditation/Journal: What holy way highway have you traveled most recently? What call did you hear? What did you have to leave behind? Was the journey rough or smooth? What transformation occurred in you?

Prayer: Your way, O LORD, is a stronghold for the upright. Reveal to me your holy way highway that I may travel it without going astray. I ask this in the name of Jesus, the way, your Son, who lives and reigns with you and the Holy Spirit forever and ever. Amen.

Along the Way

Scripture: "[The two spies] departed [Jericho] and went into the hill country and stayed there three days, until the pursuers returned. The pursuers had searched all along the way and found nothing. Then the two men came down again from the hill country. They crossed over, came to Joshua son of Nun, and told him all that had happened to them. They said to Joshua, 'Truly the LORD has given all the land into our hands; moreover all the inhabitants of the land melt in fear before us.'" (Josh 2:22–24)

Reflection: Joshua, successor leader of the Israelites following Moses, sent two spies to Jericho to search the land and bring back a report to the Israelites before they crossed the Jordan River. They are protected from the king of Jericho by Rahab, a prostitute and madame of the best little whore house in Jericho! When officials come looking for the spies, she hides them on the roof, and, once it is dark, she lowers them with a rope from a window down the city wall to freedom. They flee to the hill country for three days until their pursuers complete their search all along the way. Then, they cross the Jordan and return to Joshua to report all that happened to them and what they discovered. Later in the HB (OT) book of Joshua, he recounts how the LORD protected the people "along all the way that [they] went, and among all the peoples through whom [they] passed" (Josh 24:17b). In the HB (OT) book of Exodus, the narrator recalls how "[t]he LORD went in front of [the Israelites] in a pillar of cloud by day, to lead them along the way, and in a pillar of fire by night, to give them lights, so that they might travel by day and by night" (Exod 13:21).

The motif of the LORD protecting his people along the way is echoed over and over again throughout the Bible. It serves to assure those who take a journey that God is with them and will protect them. Standing on the right side of the Jordan River, where there is order of purpose, Joshua sends spies into the different world of Jericho. Joshua, whom God called to replace Moses, has heard the divine call to enter the land promised to Abraham, Isaac, and Jacob. He is preparing for the crossing of the river, but he needs information as to whom he will encounter on the other side. Once he receives that information from the two spies, the journey continues along the way with the people processing into the promised land (Josh 3:1—4:24). To indicate that the Israelites had been transformed by the crossing, a monument of twelve memorial stones is erected (Josh 4:1-9) and all the male Israelites, who had been born along the way of the journey, were circumcised (Josh 5:2-8).

Meditation/Journal: In what specific way(s) did God protect you on your most recent journey? In what specific way(s) did you mark the transformation that took place in you?

Prayer: Protect me, O God, along the way of my journey; for in you I take refuge; in you I place all my trust. My heart is glad, and I rejoice in you. You have shown me the path of life, and I travel it to transformation in your presence. Amen.

Successful Way

Scripture: Abraham said to his servant, "The LORD, before whom I walk, will send his angel with you and make your way successful. You shall get a wife for my son from my kindred, from my father's house." The servant said, "I came today to the spring, and said, 'O LORD, the God of my master Abraham, if now you will only make successful the way I am going! I am standing here by the spring of water—let [the young woman who comes out to draw water] be the woman whom the LORD has appointed for my master's son.'" (Gen 24:40, 42-43a, 44b)

Reflection: Abraham sends his chief servant to his hometown to find a wife for Isaac. Abraham assures the unnamed servant that the LORD will send an accompanying angel to make his servant's mission successful. In the long account of how that takes place (Gen 24:1-67), the LORD makes the way successful for his servant, who has been called by his master to go and find a wife for Isaac. After hearing the call and making preparation with camels and gifts, he takes the journey. He finds a spring and asks God to send a woman, whom he will recognize as Isaac's future wife. Rebekah appears at the spring. Then, the servant speaks to her father, Bethuel, son of Abraham's brother, Nahor, and Laban, her brother, who both declare that the giving of Rebekah to Isaac is the LORD's doing. The servant declares that "the LORD has made [his] journey successful" (Gen 24:56). The servant takes Rebekah to Isaac, and she becomes his wife.

This is named a successful way—a successful journey—because the LORD, whom Abraham serves, has made it so. The goal to be achieved was to find a wife for Isaac from among Abraham's relatives. Instead of taking the responsibility to find a woman, the servant prays to Abraham's God both to grant his success and show his steadfast love to his master, Abraham. The servant seeks to do the LORD's will by discovering whom God has appointed to be the wife of Isaac. Once Rebekah is discovered to satisfy that requirement, negotiations occur between Laban and Bethuel and Abraham's servant. Some journeys are more successful than other ones. Success implies that there is a goal to be achieved. Without that minimum, there is little to weigh in terms of success. Transformation occurs as a result of success. Abraham, his servant, Isaac, and Rebekah are all transformed as a result of the successful way.

Meditation/Journal: What has been your most successful way or journey? What made it successful? How were you and others involved in the successful way transformed?

Prayer: Send your angel to make my way successful, O LORD, as I walk before you. Blessed are you for the steadfast love and faithfulness that you bestow upon me every day of my life. Amen.

Go Your Way

Scripture: Joseph "picked out Simeon and had him bound before [the nine brothers'] eyes. Joseph then gave orders to fill their bags with grain . . . and to give them provisions for their journey. When they came to their father Jacob . . . , they told him all that had happened to them, saying [to Joseph], 'We are honest men, we are not spies. We are twelve brothers, sons of our father; one is no more, and the youngest is now with our father in the land of Canaan.' Then the man, the lord of the land [Joseph], said to us, 'By this I shall know that you are honest men: leave one of your brothers with me, take grain for the famine of your households, and go your way. Bring your youngest brother to me, and I shall know that you are not spies but honest men. Then I will release your brother to you, and you may trade in the land.'" (Gen 42:24b–25, 29, 31–34)

Reflection: The story about Joseph is the longest continuous narrative in the HB (OT) book of Genesis (37:1—50:26). Unrecognized by his ten brothers, Joseph commands nine of them to go their way. He sends them home with detailed instructions as to how to prove to him that they are not spies on their next trip to buy grain. They will need to bring with them their youngest brother, Benjamin. The command to go your way, to go home, is also found in the HB (OT) book of Ruth. After Naomi's husband and two married sons die, she is left with her two daughters-in-law: Orpah and Ruth. Because none of the women have men to care for them, Naomi tells her daughters-in-law, "Turn back, my daughters, go your way, for I am too old to have a husband" (Ruth 1:12a). Naomi is successful in sending home Orpah, but Ruth continues with her to Bethlehem, where Ruth marries Boaz and gives birth to Obed, the father of Jesse, the father of David. A third command to go home is found in the HB (OT) book of Nehemiah. After gathering before the Water Gate in Jerusalem to hear Ezra read from the book of the law of Moses, Ezra tells the people, "Go your way, eat the fat and drink sweet wine and send portions of them to those for whom nothing is prepared, for this day is holy to our LORD; and do not be grieved, for the joy of the LORD is your strength" (Neh 8:10). Then, all the people went home to eat and drink, to share their food with others, and to make great rejoicing.

At the end of a journey, we return home transformed. Joseph's nine brothers returned home transformed; they had left Simeon in Egypt, and they knew that the next time they needed to buy grain in Egypt they had to bring Benjamin with them. Their words transformed their father Jacob, who was going to be reluctant to let his youngest son accompany his brothers, who had left Simeon in Egypt. Naomi is transformed by Ruth, who remains with her when common sense dictated that she should return home. And Ruth herself was transformed by her marriage to Boaz. Nehemiah was the agent for the transformation of the Jews returned from Babylon. They had rebuilt Jerusalem's city walls and Temple; they were hearing the Mosaic Torah proclaimed which itself was transforming them. On such a holy day, they were sent home to rejoice in the transformation that had occurred and would continue to occur in them. By going on their way, all returned transformed.

Meditation/Journal: On your most recently journey, who told you to go your way? After getting home what transformation had occurred in you?

Prayer: O LORD, you are the God before whom my ancestors went their way. Open my ears to hear your call and help me prepare to take the journey to which I am summoned. Bring me home transformed in your presence. Amen.

By Way of the Sea

Scripture: "Your way [, O God,] was through the sea, your path, through the mighty waters; yet your footprints were unseen." (Ps 77:19)

Reflection: The image presented in verse 19 of Psalm 77 recalls the exodus event of the LORD driving the sea back by a strong east wind and turning it into dry land so that the Israelites journeyed through it on dry ground (Exod 14:21–31). Unlike the footprints left by the Israelites in the sand and the mud, the LORD left no footprints as he saved his chosen people. While this divine act is the pivot point of Passover, it is used often by the prophet Isaiah. He proposes the removal of gloom after Assyrian destruction when God "will make glorious the way of the sea" (Isa 9:1b). When describing a new exodus event, Isaiah, among other images, presents the LORD as one "who makes a way in the sea, a path in the mighty waters" (Isa 43:16). Similarly, in question form, the prophet asks the LORD: "Was it not you who dried up the sea, the waters of the great deep; who made the depths of the sea a way for the redeemed to cross over?" (Isa 51:10) The author of the OT (A) book of Wisdom reflects on the wisdom of the artisan, who builds a ship, "but it is your providence, O Father," writes the author, "that steers its course, because you have given it a path in the sea, and a safe way through the waves, showing that you can save from every danger, so that even a person who lacks skill may put to sea" (Wis 14:3–4).

Just as the LORD fights for Israel by providing a path through the Sea of Reeds' mighty waters, so does he do the same today for those who leave the order of their world and answer his call to take the journey. One's traveling may not be by way of the sea, but wherever one goes he or she has the assurance of God's presence, even though no footprints will be found! Passing through the mighty waters, be they crowds of people, physical exhaustion, or psychological depletion, we can be confident that our journey is guided by the Father, who makes a glorious way through the sea and saves from danger. While journeying by way of the sea, we are transformed, just like the Israelites passed from slavery in Egypt to the freedom of being God's chosen people.

Meditation/Journal: What way by the sea have you recently traveled? Were there footprints of the divine presence? From what were you redeemed? What transformation occurred in you?

Prayer: I call to mind your mighty deeds, O Father, and I remember your wonder of making a glorious way through the sea. When the waters saw you, they were afraid, but your way was through the sea with footprints unseen. By your providence steer my course today, tomorrow, and forever. Amen.

Highway

Scripture: The priests and the diviners said to the Philistines: " . . . [G]et ready a new cart and two milch cows that have never borne a yoke, and yoke the cows to the cart, but take their calves home, away from them. Take the ark of the LORD and place it on the cart . . . . Then send it off, and let it go its way. And watch; if it goes up on the way to its own land, to Beth-shemesh, then it is [the God of Israel] who has done us this great harm . . . ." The men did so; they took two milch cows and yoked them to the cart, and shut up their calves at home. They put the ark of the LORD on the cart . . . . The cows went straight in the direction of Beth-shemesh along one highway, lowing as they went; they turned neither to the right nor to the left, and the lords of the Philistines went after them as far as the border of Beth-shemesh." (1 Sam 6:7-9a, 10-12)

Reflection: The above passage from the HB (OT) book of First Samuel narrates the return of the ark of the covenant of the LORD to Israel after it had been captured by the Philistines in the second of two battles with the Israelites. After being defeated in the first battle, Israel decided to bring the ark of the LORD from Shiloh to the battlefield with the hope that God would fight for them (1 Sam 4:3-4a). While the Philistines were afraid after hearing Israel's soldiers give a mighty shout to welcome the ark into their camp, the Philistines muster their courage and defeat Israel again, capturing the ark (1 Sam 4:11a, 17, 19, 21-22). The Philistines put the ark in the temple of their god—Dagon—where it destroys Dagon's idol (1 Sam 5:1-5) and gives tumors to the people (1 Sam 5:6-7), among other things. They move it to two other cities only to experience more tumors (1 Sam 5:8-10), and then decide to return it to Israel (1 Sam 5:11-12; 6:1-6). The priests and diviners of Dagon give directions as to how it is to be returned in the above passage (1 Sam 6:7–12), and so it was set on its way to Israel (1 Sam 6:13–16). Then, once the new, ritually pure cart is back in Israel, it is set on fire to offer the two never-before-yoked cows in sacrifice to the LORD. The cows were expected by the Philistines to wander aimlessly in search of their calves, but they headed straight on the highway to Israelite territory; their behavior informed the Philistines that their suffering had been inflicted upon them by the LORD!

According to the HB (OT) book of Proverbs, "the path of the upright is a level highway" (Prov 15:19b). The LORD builds a highway for the remnant of his people (Isa 11:16); his elevated highway (Isa 49:11b) is cleared of stones and has markers directing his people (Isa 62:10). "Surely it was I who brought you through the sea, and made safe highways for you where there was no road," says the Lord (2 Esd 1:13a). When we think of highways, we may recall the Interstate system, the federal routes, the state roads, or even county ways. No matter what kind of highway we view, it is one over which we journey. The Philistines learn that bringing the ark of the covenant of the LORD into their country disrupts the order of their world. So, their suffering enables them to hear the call to prepare to return the ark on a new cart with a new yoke of cows to Israel. The milch cows take the journey out of Philistine territory and cross the border into Israel. They return their sacred cargo, which transforms Israelites, Philistines, and cart and cows into an acceptable burnt offering to God.

Meditation/Journal: What highway have you recently traveled? What was the purpose of your journey? How were you transformed?

Prayer: Hear my cry, O LORD, and save me. Direct my heart to you that I may travel the highway of your grace in service to you all the days of my life. All praise be yours now and forever. Amen.

Gateway

Scripture: " . . . [A]s I [, Ezekiel,] sat in my house, with the elders of Judah sitting before me, the hand of the Lord GOD fell upon me there. I looked, and there was a figure that looked like a human being; below what appeared to be its loins it was fire, and above the loins it was like the appearance of brightness, like gleaming amber. It stretched out the form of a hand, and took me by a lock of my head; and the spirit lifted me up between earth and heaven, and brought me in visions of God to Jerusalem, to the entrance of the gateway of the inner court that faces north, to the seat of the image of jealousy, which provokes to jealousy. And the glory of the God of Israel was there . . . . " (Ezek 8:1–4)

Reflection: In 592 BCE, after being in Babylonian captivity for six years, the prophet Ezekiel experiences a vision with a being that cannot be described in human terms; it is fire, brightness, and gleaming amber. The indescribable God brings his prophet to the gateway of the inner court of the Jerusalem Temple, where he can see the pagan idol placed there by the Babylonians. A gateway, composed of two words—gate and way—literally refers to a route through an opening in a city wall. Such gates were usually made of huge timbers covered in bronze and mounted with hinges attached to the wall so they could be opened for access to the city during the day and closed during the night to keep out enemies. In the course of time, wood gave way to iron bars, which could be lowered or raised from above. Ezekiel's vision takes him to the entrance of the most sacred area of the Temple, where he sees the glory of Israel's God, who is about to let both the Temple and the city of Jerusalem be destroyed by the Babylonians. Ezekiel uses the word *gateway* ten times (Ezek 8:3; 11:1; 26:2; 40: 3, 6, 8, 9, 11, 16, 44), more than any other biblical author. The gateway protected the now-breached inner court of the Temple. Its purpose was to protect; outside of it was the place for legal and civil events: a meeting place, a public announcement place, a market place, a deliberation place, a policy-making place, a justice place, and even a gossip place. Today, a gateway would be like a public park at lunchtime or a pub after work.

A journey takes us through many gateways. Going through a gateway is an act of leaving behind the order of our lives because we have heard a divine call—or, like Ezekiel, seen a divine vision—and prepared to take the journey that leads through new gateways. We begin by walking through the front door, a gateway to the waiting world. At the airport, we walk to the gateway, where our plane awaits us. Arriving at our destination, we walk through another gateway. The famous St. Louis Arch is spoken about as the gateway to the western United States. As Ezekiel tells us, going through a gateway is a transformative experience even after the transformation of the vision of being lifted up in spirit and brought to Jerusalem's Temple. A gateway opens us to the divine; it serves as an entrance to ongoing transformation.

Meditation/Journal: Through how many gateways have you passed today? Make a list. After each indicate what transformation occurred in you.

Prayer: Lord GOD, let your hand fall upon me and lift me up and bring me into your presence. Guide my steps through the gateways of transformation that you prepare for me. And bring me through the final gateway of death to life with you forever. Amen.

Prepare the Way

Scripture: "A voice cries out: 'In the wilderness prepare the way of the LORD, make straight in the desert a highway for our God.'" (Isa 40:3)

Reflection: The theme of building a road to Jerusalem is addressed by the prophet Isaiah originally to the Babylonian exiles returning home. Because the wilderness is the traditional place of renewal—the Israelites spent forty years there—the author of Mark's Gospel presents John the Baptizer emerging from the wilderness with the responsibility to prepare the way of renewal for Jesus Christ (Mark 1:1–4; John 1:23). The author of Matthew's Gospel enhances what he found in Mark (Matt 3:1–6; 11:10), while the author of Luke's Gospel amplifies it even more (Luke 1:76; 3:1–6; 7:27). In the Acts of the Apostles, Luke's second volume, the Way means a manner of life that leads to salvation (Acts 9:2; 18:25; 19:9, 23, 24; 24:14, 22). It is the Way of God (Acts 18:26), inferring that it is the Way of God's Messiah, Jesus.

It is a very appropriate note upon which to end this chapter. Traveling the Way of the LORD implies the ongoing life of hearing the divine call to leave behind the order of the world in order to venture into new lands. Preparation is required; it may even include building a highway in the desert! Taking the journey, however, is living the life of Jesus, an itinerant Jew of the first century who traveled from place to place announcing the presence of the kingdom of God. The Lukan Jesus explains that he is a wayfarer (Luke 4:42–43). The journey took him to Jerusalem, where he died and was transformed into resurrected life. Our transformation may not be as dramatic as his, but it is cumulative. Every time we hear and prepare to leave behind the life we have known, we discover that the journey brings us home altered, transformed, never to be the same again. The danger is listening to those who can turn us "from the way in which the LORD [our] God commanded [us] to walk" (Deut 13:5; 31:29), so that we are "unable to find [our] way" (Deut 28:29). By listening intently to and for God's word, we prepare the way for our multiple lifetime journeys that lead us home transformed.

Meditation/Journal: What are the characteristics of your manner of life on the way of your journeys? Who has prepared the way of the LORD for you? For whom have you prepared the way of the LORD?

Prayer: I listen for your voice in the wilderness of my life, O LORD, so that I can hear your call to leave behind my world and prepare to take a journey into your world. Grace me with trust that no harm will come to me, as I walk your path of renewal that results in transformation. I ask this in the name of Jesus. Amen.

7

Conclusion

Journey Themes in *The Roman Missal*

Introduction

THIS LAST CHAPTER SERVES three purposes. First, it presents a summary in seventeen reflections based on the basic outline of this book. After the first reflection on pilgrimage (as was done in the introduction to this book), we revisit the basic outline of this book. We begin with one reflection on leaving the old order behind after hearing God's call. Because it is such an

Conclusion

important part of the process, there are three reflections on answering the call by preparing to take the journey. Three reflections follow on the theme of journey, one on the theme of road, one on the theme of path, two on the theme of route, highway, gateway, one on the theme of walk, and one on the theme of the way. The chapter is concluded with two reflections on the theme of transformation, which is the goal for any pilgrimage, journey, road, path, route, highway, gateway, walk, or way.

Second, while the basic pattern of Scripture, Reflection, Meditation/Journal, and Prayer are followed in all of the entries in this chapter, the focus is on the appearance of the journey themes found in *The Roman Missal*, the book of prayers used by bishops and priests when they celebrate the Eucharist (Mass). Those themes are brought together in the Reflection of each entry, and they are footnoted for those who desire deeper reflection upon them. If the reader finds the footnotes to be cumbersome, he or she merely should ignore them.

Third, as has been noted several times and bears being said again, Binz states: "Conventual pilgrimage means going somewhere to find God in a new way; the other side of pilgrimage means going somewhere in order to bring God in a new way to that place."[1] Both long journeys to another country and short journeys down the street can be pilgrimages. According to Binz, "We can discover God's presence in the least likely places, and we can bring the presence of God to places that wait in darkness for the dawning light of the risen Lord."[2] Until we take our last breath and make our last journey through death to life, we know that all pilgrimages are incomplete. We end one journey while being hungry for more. We want more encounters with God, more experiences with Scripture, more prayer. "Pilgrimage helps us grow in our discipleship, a growth that is never complete until we reign with the Lord in glory," states Binz.[3] Journeys continue throughout our lives; each one teaches us how better to plumb the depth of our encounter with God. With the aid of Scripture, Reflection, Meditation/Journal, and Prayer we get better at leaving the old order behind after hearing God's call and answering with preparation to take the journey and come home transformed.

Gitlitz and Davidson explain, "Religious pilgrimage tends to be based on three premises: that there is an unseen power greatly superior to

---

1. Binz, *Holy Land*, 270.
2. Binz, *Holy Land*, 270–71.
3. Binz, *Holy Land*, 288.

ourselves that takes an active role in shaping our lives; that it is possible for humans to connect with that power; and that the power is especially approachable in certain privileged places."[4] "Pilgrimage is born of desire and beliefs," states Morinis. "The desire is for solution to problems of all kinds that arise within the human situation. The belief is that somewhere beyond the known world there exists a power that can make right the difficulties that appear so insoluble and intractable here and now. All one must do is journey."[5] A pilgrimage, a journey, a road, a path, a route, highway, gateway, a walk, a way changes us "inside and out," writes Poust.[6] We step out of ourselves in order to encounter God wherever he has chosen to reveal himself to us. On a pilgrimage, a journey, a road, a path, a route, highway, gateway, a walk, a way—wherever God's grace has shone with particular splendor in our lives, wherever holiness has been discovered—is an experience of being immersed in the divine. After being taken out of our usually ordered lives, we drop our guard, answer the call, prepare for and take the journey that changes us forever. According to Rohr, reordering our transformed lives "involves moving . . . toward a more spacious contemplative knowing."[7] Such a person "is the mystic, the prophet, the universal human, the saint, the whole one."[8] He or she observes the big picture, which continues to get bigger with every step he or she takes on the journey.

Pilgrimage

Scripture: Uriel said to Ezra: " . . . I will rejoice over the creation of the righteous, over their pilgrimage also, and their salvation, and their receiving their reward. As I have spoken, therefore, so it shall be." (2 Esd 8:39–40)

Reflection: As the angel Uriel (meaning "light of God") tells the prophet Ezra in the OT (A) Second Book of Esdras, he finds joy in the righteous, those people who have a healthy relationship with God. Among other things in which he rejoices is their pilgrimage to salvation. Prayers in the RM echo Uriel's words. Like those Uriel had in mind, the members of the

---

4. Gitlitz, *Pilgrimage*, 3.
5. Morinis, *Sacred Journeys*, 1.
6. Poust, *Everyday Divine*, 147.
7. Rohr, "My Story."
8. Rohr, "My Story."

Conclusion

church make their pilgrim journey through the world.[9] While it is a pilgrim church on earth[10] and all the members continue along their pilgrim journey,[11] people are formed by God's grace as they make their pilgrim way through the earthly city.[12] Indeed, God does not cease to show favor to his family on pilgrimage in this place and time.[13] Pilgrims are accompanied by the Blessed Virgin Mary, who, with a mother's love, watches the steps of those heading homeward until the day of the Lord comes.[14] Mary's assumption into heaven serves as a sign of hope and comfort for God's pilgrim people.[15] Her birth, the hope and daybreak of salvation,[16] is second only to the birth of God's Word, who took on the reality of human flesh in her immaculate womb.[17] She was overshadowed by the Holy Spirit, and Jesus, God's only begotten Son, was made incarnate.[18] This leads God's people to confess that he who was conceived in the womb of the Virgin Mary is true God and true man.[19] The birth of the Virgin's Son was the dawning of salvation;[20] God gave us through her the author of our salvation.[21] From her own body, she brought forth the Savior of the world, the author of all life.[22] In other words, God founded the salvation of humankind on the incarnation of his eternal Word.[23] We ask God to let the humanity of his only begotten Son come to our aid that we might be born again from him.[24] By imitating Mary's yes

---

9. RM, 781.
10. RM, 654, 1197.
11. RM, 214.
12. RM, 1226.
13. RM, 1034, 1225.
14. RM, 1348.
15. RM, 930.
16. RM, 943.
17. RM, 841, 843, 927, 943.
18. RM, 590, 620, 645.
19. RM, 844.
20. RM, 882, 942.
21. RM, 592.
22. RM, 637, 930.
23. RM, 802.
24. RM, 909, 1040.

to God, we hope to serve worthily the mystery of redemption,[25] especially when receiving the body of Christ, which he took from her.[26]

In the RM, we also pray to pass from the pilgrim table of the eucharistic body of Christ here on earth to the banquet of our heavenly homeland.[27] We ask God to bring us to his eternal dwelling place, where we can live with him forever, once our earthly pilgrimage is finished.[28] When our earthly pilgrimage is ended, we hope to go to and to be welcomed by Christ the Lord.[29] In the meantime, we ask God to grant safety to travelers and return to pilgrims.[30]

Meditation/Journal: At what stage is your pilgrimage to salvation? What favors have you received from God? When has God brought you safely home?

Prayer: As I make my pilgrim journey to you, O God, show me your favor by directing my footsteps with your divine grace. Grant me the accompaniment of the Blessed Virgin Mary, a sign of hope and comport, as I take my homeward steps to the eternal dwelling place to live with you forever. Amen.

Order

Scripture: " . . . Pharaoh said to Joseph, 'Since God has shown you all this, there is no one so discerning and wise as you. You shall be over my house, and all my people shall order themselves as you command; only with regard to the throne will I be greater than you.' And Pharaoh said to Joseph, 'See, I have set you over all the land of Egypt.'" (Gen 41:39–41)

Reflection: Having foreseen seven years of plenty followed by seven years of famine, Joseph, son of Jacob, is appointed by Pharaoh to reorder the land of Egypt by storing food during the years of plenty so as to have some during the years of famine. Once the storage of food is complete and the drought begins, a new order must be instituted by Joseph to make the

---

25. RM, 1040.
26. RM, 1483.
27. RM, 982.
28. RM, 779, 785, 791, 796.
29. RM, 676.
30. RM, 328.

Conclusion

supply of grain last throughout the seven years of famine. The moments of our life unfold, as stated in a prayer in the RM, according to God's good pleasure.[31] Joseph trusted without hesitation in God's fatherly providence;[32] he was urged on strongly[33] by Pharaoh's example and experienced the support of his ruler's loving intercession before him in his presence.[34]

After listening to Joseph, Pharaoh was concerned about the salvation of his people, in a way similar to the saints' concern for our salvation today.[35] With loving kindness Joseph was able to provide help to the Egyptians in both mind and body.[36] They experienced his power to save them from death.[37] As the drought years wore on, they experienced the continual increase of God's saving grace;[38] this was even more true for Joseph's father, Jacob, and his brothers, who came from Canaan to buy grain for themselves from Joseph's supplies in Egypt. In the brother they had sold into slavery, Joseph's brothers experienced God present and at work within him and them.[39] Today, Christians experience the power of Christ's cross and resurrection[40] which brings them grace and salvation in a way similar to the way Joseph saved the world.

Meditation/Journal: What order have you left behind? Make a list of the major times you altered the order of your life. What do you notice about the list?

Prayer: God of Joseph, you sent Jacob's son into slavery so that he could rise above it and save people from famine. To do so he had to alter the order of life in Egypt from consumption to storage during years of plenty. Grant me greater trust that as the moments of my life unfold at your good pleasure, I may experience your presence and power to save. Amen.

---

31. RM, 1314.
32. RM, 1319.
33. RM, 975.
34. RM, 859, 1073.
35. RM, 979, 1366.
36. RM, 1076, 1319.
37. RM, 1115.
38. RM, 1333.
39. RM, 996.
40. RM, 1330.

Call

Scripture: "Now the word of the LORD came to me [, Jeremiah,] saying, 'Before I formed you in the womb I knew you, and before you were born I consecrated you; I appointed you a prophet to the nations.'" (Jer 1:4–5)

Reflection: In the first chapter of his HB (OT) book, the prophet Jeremiah narrates that he was called by God to be a prophet before he was conceived in the womb of his mother. Jeremiah, who was a boy when he was composing this story, tells the Lord GOD that he is too young to speak. Of course, God counters his protest by declaring that he will go to all to whom he sends him, and he will speak whatever the LORD tells him to say. In the RM, we ask God that we might feel a more urgent call to work for the salvation of every living creature,[41] even if it means being called to leave Italy and minister to the immigrants in the U.S., as was St. Francis Xavier Cabrini.[42] The greater call, like that heard by Jeremiah, is issued by God; he calls human nature back to its original holiness so that we can experience on earth the gifts God promises in the new world to come.[43] In other words, God calls us back to life;[44] he calls us to eternal life.[45] Sometimes he calls a little child on the threshold of life to himself;[46] we pray that at the hour of death, he will call us and bid us to come to him.[47] Only God can make us worthy to rejoice at being called to behold him forever.[48]

Like Jeremiah, we are summoned by God to birth.[49] After that, along with others, we are summoned to appear before God.[50] We are summoned to the glory of being called a chosen race, a royal priesthood, a holy nation, a people for God's own possession.[51] We pray to be aware of the Son of God's presence among us and to experience an abundance of grace in our

---

41. RM, 1281.
42. RM, 994.
43. RM, 608.
44. RM, 630.
45. RM, 268.
46. RM, 1377.
47. RM, 1486.
48. RM, 1384.
49. RM, 628.
50. RM, 654.
51. RM, 572.

Conclusion

hearts.[52] We ask that we may be worthy to make present everywhere the living image of Jesus Christ.[53] For those who have died, who have been called to God, we ask that they might live for God,[54] in whose presence the dead are alive; we ask that for those for whom the fleeting light of this world shines no more the comfort of God's light may be theirs for all eternity.[55] Because they were faithful in this life, we ask that they have their reward in God's presence,[56] where they are called to eternal life.

Meditation/Journal: To what have you been called throughout your life? Make a list of the major times you have been called. What do you notice about the list?

Prayer: Even before I was conceived in my mother's womb, you called me to abundant life, O LORD, in your presence. Pour out the grace of your holiness on me that I may have the strength to answer your call in this life and into eternal life forever and ever. Amen.

Preparation 1

Scripture: " ... Joshua commanded the officers of the people, 'Pass through the camp and command the people: "Prepare your provisions; for in three days you are to cross over the Jordan, to go in to take possession of the land that the LORD your God gives you to possess."'" (Josh 1:10–11)

Reflection: After Moses died, Joshua became the leader of the Israelites. He traveled as second-in-command to Moses, and now, after hearing God's call, he prepares to lead the people across the Jordan River to the land promised by God to Abraham, Isaac, Jacob, and their descendants. They have three days to prepare for the second exodus crossing, not of the Sea of Reeds, but of the Jordan River. The three days indicate the divine presence; in other words, God will strengthen them with his grace.[57] He will protect with himself those who champion the faith of Israel.[58] The Israelites will

52. RM, 1284.
53. RM, 1267.
54. RM, 1399.
55. RM, 1388.
56. RM, 1399.
57. RM, 1366.
58. RM, 921.

be strengthened through the example of Joshua's invincible patience[59] to face their future trials with fortitude.[60] Thus, in the RM, we pray that God will strengthen the faith of Christians day by day with his gifts of courage and joy so that they may serve him devotedly and be worthy of still further blessings,[61] such as hope for eternal life.[62] What one receives by God's grace is designed to strengthen the hearts of all brothers and sisters.[63] The gifts bestowed on us, like those given to Joshua, purify us and strengthen us with the help they bring[64] to love God with a sincere heart and with all our strength,[65] while loving others as we love ourselves.

Then, like Joshua hastened across the Jordan River, we ask God to let us hasten with all our strength towards him, who is life.[66] Again, like Joshua and the Israelites, we ask the LORD to help us hasten toward him with minds made pure[67] and a loving heart,[68] to hasten in the way of his commandment,[69] to hasten tirelessly along the path of the gospel,[70] to hasten in the joy of Jesus Christ along the narrow way,[71] to hasten to him for healing,[72] and to hasten without stumbling to receive all the things he has promised.[73] We hasten fearlessly along God's paths, as did Israel, with our brothers and sisters, to be prepared for the delights of the eternal banquet.[74] We pray that we may hasten, alert with lighted lamps, to meet Christ, when he comes in glory,[75] even as we hasten our steps, like pilgrims advancing

---

59. RM, 945.
60. RM, 1320.
61. RM, 974, 1324.
62. RM, 1378.
63. RM, 1196, 1200.
64. RM, 1115.
65. RM, 1324.
66. RM, 1060.
67. RM, 902.
68. RM, 901.
69. RM, 1198, 1202.
70. RM, 1201.
71. RM, 1216.
72. RM, 1481.
73. RM, 486, 491.
74. RM, 1007, 1009.
75. RM, 151.

CONCLUSION

in faith, upward to God.[76] Joshua instructed the Israelites to prepare provisions to cross the Jordan River in three days; they were to hasten toward the solemn celebration of passover to come.[77]

Meditation/Journal: How long does it take for you to prepare to take a journey? What do you include on your list? In what type of hastening do you engage? To whom (or what) do you hasten?

Prayer: God of Joshua, with your grace you strengthened Mosses' successor so that he could show the Israelites how to love you with their entire being as they made their way across the Jordan River into the promised land. Strengthen my faith that I may hasten eagerly to receive all that you promise in eternal life on the other side of death. Amen.

Preparation 2

Scripture: "... Gideon went into his house and prepared a kid, and unleavened cakes from an ephah of flour; the meat he put in a basket, and the broth he put in a pot, and brought them to [the angel of the LORD] under the oak and presented them." (Judg 6:19)

Reflection: Gideon, a judge of Israel, is called by God while he is preparing wheat in a wine press to hide it from his enemy. God visibly appears to him as the angel of the LORD. To be sure that it was, indeed, God who was calling him and promising to be with him, Gideon asked the angel for a sign. The angel was to remain until Gideon went home and prepared an offering, as noted above. After bringing the offering to the angel under an oak tree and preparing it according to the divine's directions, the angel reached out the tip of his staff and fire sprang up and consumed it. The sign prompted constancy in holy faith in Gideon's heart.[78] Then, God prompted Gideon's actions with inspiration,[79] so that he could pursue what he had come to know was pleasing to God.[80] In the RM, we pray that we profess in word and deed our faith everywhere.[81] Glorying in the name of Christian, we

76. RM, 261, 981.
77. RM, 246.
78. RM, 924.
79. RM, 213.
80. RM, 1284.
81. RM, 1085.

ask God to help us show continually in our deeds the faith we profess[82] and hold fast to Christ in deeds,[83] especially his death and resurrection, by our manner of life.[84]

Just like Gideon fought battles to rid the promised land of his enemies, we seek to imitate those who fight the good fight on earth,[85] to imitate their constancy in faith,[86] to imitate the ardor of their charity,[87] to imitate their meekness,[88] to imitate their purity and love,[89] to imitate what they celebrated in the divine mysteries,[90] to imitate their accomplishments,[91] and to long for the food by which they truly lived.[92] We strive both to keep the faith and to put into practice the faith,[93] like Gideon did. We ask God that our hearts may constantly strive to cling to Christ[94] and strive for God's glory by eagerly serving others and being conformed, even to death, to Jesus.[95] By so doing, we, like Gideon who brought peace for forty years to Israel, strive to bring order and concord to the church.[96]

Meditation/Journal: As part of your preparation for a recent journey, what sign did you get from God that confirmed your call? Explain.

Prayer: God of Gideon, you sent your angel to call your servant to find a leader for your people. You confirmed his call with signs that accompanied him throughout his life. As I prepare for the next journey of my life, give me a sign of your presence and strengthen me with your Spirit. With your grace prompt my actions to do your will. Amen.

---

82. RM, 1081.
83. RM, 1042.
84. RM, 1129.
85. RM, 911.
86. RM, 862, 937, 1052.
87. RM, 877, 903.
88. RM, 810.
89. RM, 865.
90. RM, 956.
91. RM, 813.
92. RM, 866.
93. RM, 1084.
94. RM, 1350.
95. RM, 925.
96. RM, 932.

CONCLUSION

Preparation 3

Scripture: The widow of Zarephath said to Elijah, "As the LORD your God lives, I have nothing baked, only a handful of meal in a jar, and a little oil in a jug; I am now gathering a couple of sticks, so that I may go home and prepare it for myself and my son, that we may eat it, and die." (1 Kgs 17:12)

Reflection: At the word of the LORD, Elijah the prophet goes to Zarephath, where God has commanded a widow to feed him. After meeting her at the city gate, he asks her for water and food, and she tells him that she has only a little meal and oil to prepare for her son and her before they die. Elijah informs her that her jar of meal and jug of oil will not run empty until the rain falls to bring to an end the drought the land is experiencing. She trusts Elijah's word, prepares him some food, and watches as her jar and jug are replenished. In the words of the RM, by her steadfast charity, she, a Phoenician, abides in the LORD, draws life from him, and to him is drawn.[97] After her son dies and Elijah raises him to life, she professes her faith in the LORD; in other words, she is found steadfast in all her trials[98] and in confessing the name of the LORD.[99] In the RM, we pray that God will make us steadfast in faith[100] and in the face of trials steadfast in faith and in charity,[101] like the widow, that we may have our reward in the life to come.[102]

The act of preparing for a journey enables us to grow in wisdom and grace,[103] in spiritual things,[104] in sincere love of God on earth until the end of our lives,[105] in love of the truth,[106] in faith and holiness according to God's will,[107] and in knowledge of God.[108] We ask God to renew our growth in

---

97. RM, 1058.
98. RM, 950, 1055.
99. RM, 1052.
100. RM, 1066.
101. RM, 872.
102. RM, 1395.
103. RM, 898, 1083.
104. RM, 1293.
105. RM, 857, 910, 1094, 1095.
106. RM, 1277.
107. RM, 839, 1085, 1248.
108. RM, 931.

heavenly life[109] that we may rejoice to behold him for all eternity in heaven.[110] While preparing for our journey, we seek unceasing growth of God's church[111] that all people may grow strong in communion with Christ's Spirit, in eager communion with each other, and in love for one another.[112] We hope to receive new growth in freedom through our preparation.[113] We pray that the church will grow by increase in the number of people who believe in God[114] and so build up the heavenly Jerusalem in numbers of faithful people.[115] We ask the LORD to preserve faithfully his gift of the spirit of adoption, by which we are called, and truly are now, his children.[116] That is what the widow did for Elijah, as she prepared her last bit of food for him.

Meditation/Journal: In what areas of your life did you experience growth during your preparation for your most recent journey? Identify the area and name the growth that occurred.

Prayer: God of Elijah, you sent your prophet to the widow of Zarephath, who prepared her last handful of meal and little bit of oil into a cake for him. Little did she know that her preparation of a little would result in an abundance. Through my preparation, grant me the grace to abide in you, to draw life from you, and to you be drawn all the days of my life. Amen.

Journey 1

Scripture: The Israelites "set out from the mount of the LORD three days' journey with the ark of the covenant of the LORD going before them three days' journey, to seek out a resting place for them, the cloud of the LORD being over them by day when they set out from the camp." (Num 10:33–34)

Reflection: The journey narrated in the HB (OT) book of Numbers is filled with divine presence. First, the Israelites set out from the mountain of the

---

109. RM, 1094.
110. RM, 1094.
111. RM, 1363.
112. RM, 1128, 1260.
113. RM, 1270.
114. RM, 977.
115. RM, 988.
116. RM, 824, 955.

Conclusion

LORD, known as Sinai and Horeb, where God appeared to them in fire, thunder, and lightning. The Holy One's presence is signified by the number three—stated twice in the above passage—the ark of the covenant, and the cloud. Put simply, as they make their journey to the promised land, the Israelites are immersed in the LORD's presence. This is why in the RM we pray that on life's journey we may be effective in good works and rich in the gifts of hope, faith, and charity.[117] We ask God to help us proceed happily on the journey toward him which we began a long time ago.[118] Like St. Francis Xavier, who, as a missionary, journeyed to distant lands,[119] we journey to our heavenly homeland.[120] According to the RM, God calls people to journey to him from this world;[121] thus, we pray that he will grant the dying a peaceful journey to his kingdom and lead them to the gift of eternal life.[122] The dying have food for the journey, the eucharist, which strengthens them so that they go to the eternal table of Christ.[123] Like the Israelites immersed in God's presence on their journey to the promised land, we are impelled towards higher goods.[124] We press forward eagerly to celebrate the paschal mystery, following in the Savior's footsteps to the place he has entered before us.[125] As we proceed to the house of God to encounter Christ,[126] we go forth from this world in peace and trust to meet the Lord, while acknowledging other servants who have gone before us with the sign of faith.[127] Just like God protected the Israelites with his presence in the cloud, so does he go before us with heavenly light.[128]

By perseverance in obeying the divine will, the Israelites were able to make their way through the desert to the promised land.[129] Through

---

117. RM, 680.
118. RM, 1265.
119. RM, 1007.
120. RM, 1073.
121. RM, 1371, 1374.
122. RM, 1136.
123. RM, 1372.
124. RM, 255.
125. RM, 159, 243, 431.
126. RM, 816.
127. RM, 642, 817, 821, 1317.
128. RM, 189.
129. RM, 1267.

our perseverance in holy living,[130] in love of God and others,[131] in keeping God's commandments,[132] in confessing faith,[133] God draws us ever closer to salvation.[134] That is why we pray that God, from whom faith draws perseverance and weakness draws strength,[135] will give us perseverance in his service,[136] just like he did for his people of old. Then, we, like they, can persevere in devotion to him and stand ever firm before him.[137] We can persevere as one heart and one soul[138] in constant thanksgiving for his presence,[139] imitating the Israelites and Christ,[140] and receive the rewards God has promised to those who persevere.[141]

Meditation/Journal: What were the signs of God's presence with you on your most recent journey? In what specific ways have you persevered in holy living?

Prayer: LORD God, you were present to your chosen people in the ark and the cloud. You have made your presence in human flesh in your Son, Jesus Christ. Awaken me to all the signs of your presence with me, as I proceed happily on the journey towards you already long ago begun. Amen.

Journey 2

Scripture: " . . . [I]f you have been raised with Christ, seek the things that are above, where Christ is seated at the right hand of God. Set your minds on things that are above, not on things that are on earth, for you have died, and your life is hidden with Christ in God." (Col 3:1–3)

---

130. RM, 264.
131. RM, 906, 1114, 1256.
132. RM, 904.
133. RM, 826, 847, 863.
134. RM, 1352.
135. RM, 1062.
136. RM, 832.
137. RM, 860.
138. RM, 973.
139. RM, 876.
140. RM, 1107.
141. RM, 1058.

Conclusion

Reflection: In the second-generation Pauline letter to the Colossians, the author identifies seeking as one aspect of a journey. After one dies and rises with Christ in baptism, then a person seeks salvation that comes from above, that is, from the heavenly realm, where after he died and was raised, Jesus was seated at his Father's right hand of power. Minds are also to be focused on things above and not on the things of earth; existence has been transformed by the death and resurrection of Christ. Likewise, those who have been baptized have had their existence transformed; they have died with Christ in baptism, and they have been raised with him. Now, they have a new identify; they are alive with divine life found in Christ and God! That is why in the RM, we ask God to prompt our hearts always to seek and treasure the things that are his.[142] By seeking him above all things,[143] we bear the likeness of the new man and new woman in the world.[144] By seeking to do God's will,[145] we seek what is divine[146] and a livelier faith.[147] In other words, we seek the author of heavenly love[148] and his Son, Jesus Christ, that we may love our neighbor in deeds and in truth.[149] Our prayer is that we always seek God with diligent love and find him in our daily service with sincere faith.[150] On our journey, we seek God by desiring him, and by finding him, come to rest.[151] We pray that those who seek the truth may joyfully find their God, and that his faithful people may persevere in confessing him on their journey.[152]

While we travel through life, we hope to reflect the pattern of God's love,[153] while setting out in haste to meet his Son and reflecting among all humanity the image of his divine goodness along with the image of Christ to all people.[154] As the author of Colossians urges his readers to set their

---

142. RM, 976, 1043.
143. RM, 1000.
144. RM, 1109.
145. RM, 898.
146. RM, 262.
147. RM, 1019.
148. RM, 938.
149. RM, 943.
150. RM, 803.
151. RM, 326.
152. RM, 1022.
153. RM, 1112.
154. RM, 146, 804, 995.

minds on things above, we pray to be released from earthly attachments so that our riches are in God alone.[155] In all confidence, we follow the Christ,[156] who calls us to follow him,[157] journeying faithfully in his footsteps[158] and petitioning God never to cease to prompt us to follow more closely in his Son's footsteps[159] with a generous heart and a willing spirit.[160] Taking our cue from Colossians, we renounce the things of this world,[161] we bear our cross,[162] and we seek to follow Christ in faithful devotion.[163] We have multiple examples in the saints who merited to hold firm in following Christ.[164] They give us examples of how to seek God,[165] of holy living,[166] of prayer and love,[167] of gentleness in charity and service of our neighbor,[168] of missionary zeal,[169] of teaching,[170] and of willingly spending our lives working for the honor and unity of the church.[171] We pray that as we follow the teachings of the Christian life, we may know God's help in every trial[172] and be led by him to attain his promise of heaven,[173] while following Christ our master with our neighbor into God's presence.[174]

Meditation/Journal: On your journey, when have you recently died and been raised transformed? On your journey, where have you found God? Make a list of the major places. What do you notice about the list?

155. RM, 1109.
156. RM, 676.
157. RM, 787.
158. RM, 274, 850.
159. RM, 1266.
160. RM, 1127.
161. RM, 1263.
162. RM, 1283.
163. RM, 1204.
164. RM, 953.
165. RM, 901.
166. RM, 1079, 1113.
167. RM, 805.
168. RM, 810.
169. RM, 998.
170. RM, 933.
171. RM, 994.
172. RM, 875.
173. RM, 988, 1036.
174. RM, 1112.

Prayer: While I treasure the things that are yours, heavenly Father, I seek you always. Grant me a share in your divine goodness that enables me to follow in your Son's footsteps in holy living and be transformed day by day by your love. I ask this in the name of Jesus Christ, my Lord. Amen.

Journey 3

Scripture: "From [the Word's] fullness we have all received, grace upon grace. The law indeed was given through Moses; grace and truth came through Jesus Christ." (John 1:16–17)

Reflection: Instead of thinking about grace as a thing, we need to think of grace as a verb; grace is the act of God sharing himself with people. The greatest outpouring of grace was the Word becoming flesh, the incarnation; from that fullness, according to the author of John's Gospel, we have received grace upon grace. The divine life the Word received from the Father has become a ceaseless river of grace after grace poured out as a blessing[175] and making people joint heirs to the life of grace.[176] While the Torah was given through Moses, God's own divine life came through Jesus Christ. That is why in the RM we ask God to send his grace at all times to us on our journey, so that it goes before us and follows after us.[177] In that way we can draw upon the fullness of God's grace,[178] which, through Christ, we merit to receive.[179] While our journey is a time of grace,[180] it is supported by the perpetual help of God's own self, and it is resplendent with the glory of our lives acceptable to God.[181] In other words, we are made a temple for God's grace, a dwelling place for God's glory.[182] Nurtured by grace[183] and relying solely on the hope of receiving it,[184] we can be so fashioned by it that

---

175. RM, 1181.
176. RM, 1182.
177. RM, 488.
178. RM, 1258.
179. RM, 998, 1041.
180. RM, 1271.
181. RM, 990, 1037.
182. RM, 990.
183. RM, 1099.
184. RM, 465.

we become a dwelling place pleasing to God.[185] Indeed, according to John's Gospel, God has been pleased to save us with his grace.[186] We ask God to help us experience its continued increase for our salvation.[187] The Blessed Virgin Mary is an example of one who was endowed with the rich fullness of grace, often referred to as prevenient grace,[188] to become a worthy mother and dwelling place for God's Son.[189]

While we journey, we ask God to keep bestowing the grace of his light upon us, so that we may have a true understanding of what is correct in his eyes and boldly live it.[190] We ask God to renew the sanctifying grace he gives in the church;[191] it is a blessed gift with which he assists his servants[192] by making new the wonders of grace in their hearts.[193] Grace enables people to serve God,[194] to attain his protection,[195] to be kept safe,[196] to be witnesses to charity,[197] and to find relief through his mercy.[198] It is by the grace of God's mercy that commands the names of his servants to be inscribed in the book of life.[199] Grace strengthens husband and wife in marriage;[200] by providence and grace God brings the birth of children into the marriage and brings them to rebirth in baptism.[201] Grace brings growth in membership in the church and an abundance of virtues.[202] We pray that such divine grace may spread through the hearts of all who believe in God,[203] so that their first

---

185. RM, 466, 1095, 1221.
186. RM, 1308.
187. RM, 869, 1041.
188. RM, 1016.
189. RM, 1013, 1016.
190. RM, 1249.
191. RM, 1278.
192. RM, 1122.
193. RM, 992.
194. RM, 1155, 1160, 1251.
195. RM, 1218, 1454.
196. RM, 1131.
197. RM, 1111, 1177.
198. RM, 1320.
199. RM, 1373.
200. RM, 1180.
201. RM, 1179.
202. RM, 1351.
203. RM, 1344.

fruits may be transformed by more grace into a plentiful harvest.[204] With great trust in God's grace from on high,[205] we hope to obtain the grace of heavenly blessing,[206] that is, eternal glory.[207] We pray for an increase in saving grace,[208] for an abundance of grace[209] poured out on God's servants[210] that gladden them in great measure[211] and results in unceasing growth.[212] We petition God to pour out the grace of the Holy Spirit upon us,[213] so we can walk worthily in the vocation to which he has called us[214] and fill the whole earth with his grace.[215] It is by the grace of the Holy Spirit that God has filled the hearts of his faithful people with countless gifts of charity, and so we ask him to grant health of mind and body to his servants.[216]

Meditation/Journal: On your journey, when have you experienced the fullness of grace that went before you and followed after you? Make a list. What do you notice about the list?

Prayer: God of all grace, from the fullness of your Word, Jesus Christ, I have received grace upon grace. Never cease to fill me with your divine life that leads me onward to the glory of your kingdom, where you live and reign with your Son and the Holy Spirit forever and ever. Amen.

Road

Scripture: "[Moses] ... said to Korah and all his company, 'In the morning the LORD will make known who is his, and who is holy, and who will be

204. RM, 1207.
205. RM, 1219.
206. RM, 1310.
207. RM, 1096.
208. RM, 1103.
209. RM, 1101, 1138, 1146, 1252.
210. RM, 1184.
211. RM, 1119.
212. RM, 1036.
213. RM, 1309.
214. RM, 1272.
215. RM, 1349.
216. RM, 1310.

allowed to approach him; the one whom he will choose he will allow to approach him.'" (Num 16:5)

Reflection: While on the road to the promised land, Moses must deal with rebellion among the Israelites. The HB (OT) book of Numbers narrates the rise of Korah and two hundred fifty Israelite men who claimed the right to act as priests in offering incense and sacrifices at the altar. Moses' opposition claims that all Israelites are holy and worthy to serve as priests, not just Moses and Aaron. What Korah and his followers fail to note is that God chose Moses and Aaron to approach him. The next day, with censers in hand, the rebels approach the glory of the LORD, which appeared to the whole congregation of Israel. The ground opened, all of them were swallowed, and the ground closed over them. Thus, the LORD decreed that only Aaron's descendants could approach him to offer incense. In the RM, we ask God to give us what we need in the present age that we may become a sacrifice acceptable to him for the salvation of the world and prepared for the gifts that are eternal.[217]

Through the merits of the death and resurrection of Jesus Christ, we may approach with confidence the throne of grace.[218] Jesus appeared in our mortal nature though invisible in his own divine nature.[219] The one begotten before all ages began to exist in time, making us new by the glory of his immortal nature.[220] The only begotten Son, eternal with God in glory, appeared in a human body, truly sharing our flesh.[221] In other words, a holy exchange occurred; our human frailty was assumed by God's Word, and we were made eternal.[222] The one who was in the form of God emptied himself to become one of us.[223] What Korah and his followers sought to attain was brought about by God's Son. While traveling the road of life, we approach the font of rebirth[224] and we ask God to help us know what must be done so we can bring it to completion.[225] By carrying out with one accord the

---

217. RM, 489, 952.
218. RM, 431.
219. RM, 540, 544.
220. RM, 540, 544.
221. RM, 637.
222. RM, 534, 542.
223. RM, 610.
224. RM, 369.
225. RM, 905.

CONCLUSION

works of holiness on the road of life,[226] we seek to be constant in fulfilling the divine will.[227] We pray that God will confirm us in our resolve to do his will,[228] in the profession of his truth,[229] and in love of our neighbor.[230] As we travel the road of life, we ask him to shield us with the protection of his lovingkindness[231] so that his gifts are kept safe in us.[232] Working in harmony with his will in all things, we glory in being truly his.[233] And while holding more closely day by day to Christ, we hope to be coheirs in his kingdom, possessing the riches of grace.[234]

Meditation/Journal: While you travel life's roads, in what ways do you approach God? Make a list of the major ways you approach God. What do you notice about the list?

Prayer: Almighty God, your only begotten Son appeared in my mortal nature in order to renew me in your immortal nature. Pour the riches of your grace upon me that I am able to do your will in all things and, while on the road of life, glory in being truly yours today, tomorrow, and forever. Amen.

Path

Scripture: " . . . [L]o, the one who forms the mountains, creates the wind, reveals his thoughts to mortals, makes the morning darkness, and treads on the heights of the earth—the LORD, the God of hosts, is his name!" (Amos 4:13)

Reflection: After recounting Israel's stubbornness, the prophet Amos presents a series of divine judgments that have failed to convince the people of their injustices. The LORD promises his final judgment for Israel's failure to reform, stating, " . . . [P]repare to meet your God, O Israel!" (Amos 4:12) Then follows the statement of authority which gives God the right to judge:

226. RM, 1199.
227. RM, 1017.
228. RM, 1285.
229. RM, 877, 1055, 1100, 1132.
230. RM, 1044, 1110.
231. RM, 252.
232. RM, 891.
233. RM, 993.
234. RM, 876, 1107.

He made the mountains; he creates the wind; he reveals his thoughts to people; he makes the early morning darkness; and he treads the paths over the earth. According to Amos, he is named the LORD, the God of hosts. He walks the paths of the highest of the three stories of earth, while his people walk the paths of the middle of the three stories of earth. This is echoed in the RM; we ask God to help us tread the paths of life on earth and one day drink at the stream of heavenly delights.[235] Unlike the Israelites, we hope never to stray from the paths of life;[236] to do this we need divine protection in our weakness to help us tread the path of salvation as we make our way to the LORD.[237] We tread the path of virtue[238] and the path of humility to heavenly glory.[239] We ask God to lead the church along the paths of time,[240] while helping her members understand the path they need to follow and, by following it, obtain life everlasting in eternity.[241]

Our prayer is that God will mercifully guide our footsteps in his paths[242] that we may advance boldly along the way of salvation[243] and joyfully along the way of love.[244] Advancing without hinderance towards the hope of glory,[245] we strive bravely to overcome all things for the sake of him who loved us.[246] Through our progress in learning, we come to a deeper knowledge and love of God,[247] pursuing in freedom of heart the things that are his,[248] praying that he will never let us be parted from him,[249] while offering our very lives to him[250] on earth's paths, while preparing for heaven's walkways.

235. RM, 935.
236. RM, 402.
237. RM, 1101.
238. RM, 816.
239. RM, 986.
240. RM, 781.
241. RM, 387, 962.
242. RM, 1269.
243. RM, 961, 1042, 1279.
244. RM, 1109, 1279.
245. RM, 1324.
246. RM, 1054.
247. RM, 995.
248. RM, 492.
249. RM, 668.
250. RM, 925.

Conclusion

Meditation/Journal: Upon what paths have you been guided by the LORD? Make a list of the major paths. What do you notice about the list?

Prayer: You form the mountains, you create the wind, you reveal your thoughts to people, you make the morning darkness, and you tread on the heights of the earth, O LORD, God of hosts. Guide my footsteps on your path on earth that I may be found worthy to walk with you in heaven. Amen.

Route, Highway, Gateway 1

Scripture: Jesus said: "Enter through the narrow gate; for the gate is wide and the road is easy that leads to destruction, and there are many who take it. For the gate is narrow and the road is hard that leads to life, and there are few who find it." (Matt 7:13–14)

Reflection: The image used by the Matthean Jesus near the end of his sermon on the mount is that of a city gate through which people were able to enter a walled town. According to Jesus, entering the kingdom of God is like passing through a narrow entrance while walking over a hard road of life's tribulations. Many people prefer the wide gate while traveling the paved road without life's stresses and hardships. The former way leads to life in the kingdom; the latter way leads to destruction. According to the Matthean Jesus, entering the kingdom of God is difficult, and only a few manage to find the gate. In the RM, we ask God to lead us to life on high, and we ask Jesus to go before us to lead us and to go behind us to guard us.[251] We pray that God will lead us to grace through a devout way of life.[252] We petition God to lead us in sincerity of heart to attain the holy things to come,[253] while now we ask him to lead us to a worthy celebration of the sacred mysteries.[254] Like God led his people, Israel, through the desert,[255] we ask him to lead us to what is right[256] and onward to the gifts of salvation.[257]

---

251. RM, 1135.
252. RM, 234, 1122.
253. RM, 234.
254. RM, 977.
255. RM, 781.
256. RM, 470.
257. RM, 235.

As we travel the hard road through the narrow gate, we need God to lead us to true justice and lasting peace,[258] to growth in charity,[259] to the fullness of grace,[260] to bear witness, like Peter, to Jesus,[261] and to new life.[262]

According to the RM, God led Jesus through his passion and death on the cross to new life over the hard road and through the narrow gate,[263] and Jesus led the human race out of walking in darkness to the radiance of faith.[264] Every time we recite the Lord's Prayer, we ask God to lead us not into temptation,[265] while we also ask him to lead those he has imbued with heavenly mysteries,[266] our brothers and sisters, to the blessedness and joys of eternal life.[267] The God who leads us graciously to gifts on high through the narrow gate[268] brings us to what he promises for all eternity.[269] In other words, God leads us over the hard road and through the narrow gate of his kingdom to where he calls us.[270]

Meditation/Journal: To what places has God led you? Make a list of the major places. What do you notice about the list?

Prayer: Holy God, your Son, Jesus Christ, has shown us the way to your kingdom. As he goes before me to lead me and behind me to guard me, grant me the grace to stay on the hard road that passes through the narrow gate to the eternal city, where you live forever and ever. Amen.

---

258. RM, 893.
259. RM, 470.
260. RM, 355, 546.
261. RM, 1362.
262. RM, 258.
263. RM, 778, 784, 790, 796.
264. RM, 248.
265. RM, 663.
266. RM, 399, 408, 414, 422, 428, 439, 476.
267. RM, 183, 827, 967.
268. RM, 232.
269. RM, 268.
270. RM, 286.

CONCLUSION

Route, Highway, Gateway 2

Scripture: Jesus said to his disciples, "When the Spirit of truth comes, he will guide you into all the truth; for he will not speak on his own, but will speak whatever he hears, and he will declare to you the things that are to come." (John 16:13)

Reflection: Coming from the inserted discourse material in John 14:1–17:26, the above verse refers to the ongoing revelation of God. Before Jesus, God revealed himself to the patriarchs and matriarchs, then the Hebrews, then the Israelites, then the Jews. In the fullness of time, God revealed himself in the person of his Son, Jesus, who became human. The Johannine Jesus informs his followers that the Spirit will continue God's revelation by guiding them to deeper truth and deeper meaning into what has already happened, while pointing forward to what will flow from the event of Jesus. In other words, God's revelation continues from the death and resurrection of Jesus to our own day. In his letter to the Galatians, Paul echoes the Johannine author, exhorting his readers, "If we live by the Spirit, let us also be guided by the Spirit" (Gal 5:25).

Thus, in the RM, we ask God to lend us ready help in our weakness.[271] We ask God to guide us unfailingly through the present life[272] and to sustain us in many ways.[273] We also pray that the church will be guided by her apostolic protectors[274] and by God's eternal design.[275] Along the way, we call upon God to be the protector of all who hope in him[276] through the action of the Spirit. We need God's constant protection with grace.[277] We invoke St. Joseph as our protector on earth,[278] and God's angels so that we may advance boldly along the way of salvation.[279]

Meditation/Journal: To what truths has the Spirit guided you? Make a list of the major truths. What do you notice about the list?

271. RM, 848.
272. RM, 196, 239, 470, 1310.
273. RM, 195, 201.
274. RM, 1359.
275. RM, 250.
276. RM, 253.
277. RM, 1156, 1161, 1176.
278. RM, 1356.
279. RM, 1353.

Prayer: Give me unfailing guidance with your Spirit, O LORD. Sustain me on my journeys and protect me with your grace all along the way of salvation in this life to the life to come. Amen.

Walk

Scripture: "[The LORD] has told you, O mortal, what is good; and what does the LORD require of you but to do justice, and to love kindness, and to walk humbly with your God?" (Mic 6:8)

Reflection: In one verse, the prophet Micah offers a summary of most prophetic thought. There are three elements in the summary addressed to mortals. The first, justice, describes the fairness and equality that should govern all social relationship. The second, kindness or mercy—loyalty or integrity—refers to fulfilling social responsibilities responsibly. And the third, walking humbly with God, refers to a way of life that is opposed to the exploitation of power. What interests us here is walking humbly with God, who always walks with us on the journey of life.[280] And so we pray to walk faithfully in his presence[281] and to walk before him with a sincere heart.[282] Keeping in mind that we walk amid passing things,[283] we petition God to make us walk worthily and faithfully in our vocation in order to seek him in all things.[284] By doing so, we walk the path of salvation that he traces for us with deeds of devoted service.[285]

The way of life that Micah indicates—walking humbly with our God—means that we walk always as children of light;[286] we walk in the light of God's truth[287] with faith and hope.[288] We walk eagerly in charity with our neigh-

---

280. RM, 776, 782, 788, 794.
281. RM, 1087.
282. RM, 324.
283. RM, 139, 140, 143, 147, 150, 154, 157.
284. RM, 906, 924, 1008, 1107, 1366.
285. RM, 801, 878, 1079.
286. RM, 932.
287. RM, 822.
288. RM, 784.

Conclusion

bor[289] in the pathways of the gospel[290] even through the shadow of death[291] to newness of life.[292] While we walk humbly with God, he does not cease to spur us on to possess a more abundant life.[293] In other words, we run the course of this present life under his guidance so that we may happily attain life without end.[294] Thus, we do well to set our course to attain the redemption he promises.[295] Then, after running the race of this present life[296]—that is, walking humbly with our God—we set our goal to be victors,[297] who run forth to meet Christ.[298] Our prayer is that through walking and running, we may stand firm in faith and remain constant in hope of the gospel preached,[299] while knowing the protection of lasting peace[300] until the hour when we stand before the God with whom we have humbly walked.[301]

Meditation/Journal: When have you and God walked together? Make a list of the major walks. What changes in your way of life were the result of those walks?

Prayer: O LORD, you have told me what is good and what you require of me: to do justice, and to love kindness, and to walk humble with you, my God. Always walk with me on my journey of life that I may follow my vocation on the path of salvation you have given to me and come to newness of life in your presence. Amen.

---

289. RM, 256, 1364.
290. RM, 1044.
291. RM, 249.
292. RM, 1064, 1126, 1128.
293. RM, 760.
294. RM, 1027.
295. RM, 234.
296. RM, 674.
297. RM, 598.
298. RM, 139.
299. RM, 1084.
300. RM, 991.
301. RM, 764.

Way

Scripture: "While [a slave-girl who had a spirit of divination] followed Paul and us, she would cry out, 'These men are slaves of the Most High God, who proclaims to you a way of salvation.' She kept doing this for many days. But Paul, very much annoyed, turned and said to the spirit, 'I order you in the name of Jesus Christ to come out of her.' And it came out that very hour." (Acts 16:17–18)

Reflection: Most of the Acts of the Apostles is written in third-person narrative. However, there are so-called "we" sections—beginning at Acts 16:10—which change to first-person plural accounts. The account of the slave girl with a spirit of divination given above is one of those first-person plural stories. We have no way of knowing who the "us" is. What we can recognize is the Lukan irony: A slave possessed by a spirit proclaims the truth about Paul and his companions being slaves of God, who, through Paul and "us," proclaims a way of salvation to those willing to hear. Ultimately, in imitation of Jesus, Paul exorcises the girl in the name of Jesus, and the spirit leaves her; she has experienced the way of salvation. That is why in the RM we pray that the way of salvation may lie open before us[302] and that God will direct others along the way of salvation.[303] Since God has opened the way to eternal life,[304] we follow the way he desires for us.[305] As we know from John's Gospel, Jesus is the way, the truth, and the life (John 14:6) for us;[306] he is the way of truth that leads us to God.[307] Thus, living in a manner worthy of the gospel of Christ,[308] we, like Paul and his companions, live bravely in confessing the Most High God,[309] while praying that God's promise of eternal redemption may be of help to us both now and for the life to come,[310] where life is changed, not ended.[311]

---

302. RM, 1008.
303. RM, 1124.
304. RM, 578.
305. RM, 402.
306. RM, 1136.
307. RM, 184, 787.
308. RM, 1322, 1365.
309. RM, 1053.
310. RM, 1082.
311. RM, 622.

Conclusion

We attempt to live a worthy way of life[312] by asking God to grant fraternal communion and spiritual freedom to all who set out to imitate Jesus by following the narrow way,[313] while we make our way by means of God's heavenly gifts.[314] One of those heavenly gifts is the body and blood of Christ veiled under the species of bread and wine.[315] As wayfarers, we hope to live by that sacrament in serenity and moderation.[316] For it is in God in whom we live and move and have our being,[317] and, while still in this life, receive his holy sacrament as food for our journey.[318] We pray that God will direct the wavering hearts of his flock,[319] his faithful people, his servants, to himself in the way of eternal salvation.[320] We acknowledge that God directs our life in all its moments,[321] whether in tribulation or in prosperity,[322] just like he directed the slave-girl to proclaim him the Most High God, who, through Paul and his companions, preached a way of salvation.

Meditation/Journal: When have you experienced the way of salvation? Make a list of the major times. What changes in your way of life were the result of those experiences?

Prayer: Most High God, you open before me the way of salvation by making your Son, Jesus Christ, the way, the truth, and the life. Grant me the grace to live a life worthy of his gospel that I, a wayfarer, may use wisely your heavenly gifts to arrive safely in your kingdom. Amen.

Transformation 1

Scripture: " . . . [S]ince we are surrounded by so great a cloud of witnesses, let us also lay aside every weight and the sin that clings so closely, and let

---

312. RM, 399, 408, 414, 418, 422, 428.
313. RM, 1266.
314. RM, 419.
315. RM, 1483.
316. RM, 830, 1106.
317. RM, 582.
318. RM, 1397.
319. RM, 239, 262.
320. RM, 233, 879, 904, 965, 1071.
321. RM, 1409.
322. RM, 992.

us run with perseverance the race that is set before us, looking to Jesus the pioneer and perfecter of our faith, who for the sake of the joy that was set before him endured the cross, disregarding its shame, and has taken his seat at the right hand of the throne of God." (Heb 12:1–2)

Reflection: The anonymous author of the letter to the Hebrews reminds his readers that they are surrounded by a large crowd of people who have remained faithful to Jesus. He exhorts them to throw off the encumbrance of sin in order to run with perseverance the race of faith that has been set before them. The model race-runner is Jesus, who is both pioneer—the inventor—and the perfecter—skilled worker—of faith; Jesus endured the cross and the shame associated with it in order to be transformed for the joy of sitting at the right hand of God's throne. Because the Son of God is a fitting model of transformation, we know that it is by the power of God's Holy Spirit that the Father comes unfailingly to people's aid.[323] Amid the uncertainties of the world, we need help to cling with all our heart to the things of heaven.[324] God is pleased to create us in his image and to adopt us as his own in baptism, and so we ask him to give us a share in his eternal inheritance.[325] While awaiting the final transformation for which we long, we receive God's consolation in this life, not losing hope of what he has promised us for eternity.[326] We see Jesus as our example; as we are beset by the trials of this life, we hear about Jesus, who for the sake of the joy to come, endured the cross to be transformed into eternal rest.[327] Our prayer is that we may merit by endurance an eternal prize,[328] while completing in ourselves what is lacking in the sufferings of Christ.[329] We finish the race we have begun, persevering in the resolve we have made our own,[330] so that the moment when we depart this world in death,[331] we may be transformed into the joys of eternal life, just like Christ,[332] to behold God for eternity.[333]

323. RM, 1343.
324. RM, 1104.
325. RM, 828, 1389.
326. RM, 1106.
327. RM, 1316.
328. RM, 1001.
329. RM, 949.
330. RM, 1203.
331. RM, 1318.
332. RM, 418, 1329.
333. RM, 922.

Conclusion

In other words, the ending of present things opens to the beginning of things to come.[334] That is transformation.

Christian hope draws us onward,[335] away from earthly and unruly desires,[336] as stated in Hebrews. It draws us to God's Son, Jesus.[337] We are drawn nearer and nearer to the sacrifice of salvation[338] and the company of heaven,[339] even as we petition God to draw nearer to us, his servants,[340] and draw us nearer to him.[341] It is he who gathers what is scattered and keeps together what he has gathered.[342] He never ceases to gather a people scattered throughout the world[343] to himself[344] through the blood of the cross of his Son and the power of the Spirit.[345] God gathers his children to the table of his Son and makes them one body of Christ with the Holy Spirit.[346] Those who have been transformed through final death are gathered into the company of God's chosen ones;[347] they have run the race with perseverance, looking to Jesus, the pioneer and perfecter of their faith.

Meditation/Journal: When have you been transformed? Make a list of the major experiences of transformation. What changes took place in you as a result of those transformations?

Prayer: God of Jesus, you surround me with a great cloud of faithful witnesses. As I run with perseverance the race you set before me, turn me towards your Son, the pioneer and perfecter of faith, who leads me through the uncertainties and trials of this life to your throne, O God, forever. Amen.

334. RM, 1375.
335. RM, 433.
336. RM, 244, 393.
337. RM, 504.
338. RM, 962.
339. RM, 1105.
340. RM, 478.
341. RM, 811.
342. RM, 322.
343. RM, 654.
344. RM, 650.
345. RM, 586.
346. RM, 660, 648, 771.
347. RM, 1382.

Transformation 2

Scripture: Moses said to the elders of Israel: "Go, select lambs for your families, and slaughter the passover lamb. Take a bunch of hyssop, dip it in the blood that is in the basin, and touch the lintel and the two doorposts with the blood in the basin. None of you shall go outside the door of your house until morning. For the LORD will pass through to strike down the Egyptians; when he sees the blood on the lintel and on the two doorposts, the LORD will pass over that door and will not allow the destroyer to enter your houses to strike you down." (Exod 12:21–23)

Reflection: The Israelites are transformed by the blood of a slaughtered lamb sprinkled with twigs of hyssop on the lintel and the two doorposts of their homes. Hyssop, an aromatic bush used for ritual purification, distinguishes the Israelites' homes from the Egyptians' homes to the LORD, who protects the Israelites from the destroyer. The transforming occurs as the LORD passes over the doors marked with lamb's blood. The Israelites are transformed from imminent death to abundant life. They pass over from old to new.[348] Once they escape Egypt, they will pass dry-shod through the Red Sea,[349] again from imminent death executed by Pharaoh and his military might to abundant life. They become a model of how to deal with the things of this passing world while holding to the things that endure eternally.[350] In other words, the passovers of the Israelites demonstrate how to be transformed from realities foreshadowed to heavenly realities.[351]

While passover is marked in the Christian church by the death of Jesus, who is transformed into risen life, it is also celebrated for those who have died, those who have passed from this world.[352] We pray that at the hour of our death we may pass over safely to God.[353] In other words, we pray to pass through the shadows of this world to reach the brightness of our eternal home,[354] a dwelling place of light and peace,[355] the glory of the

---

348. RM, 254.
349. RM, 354, 377.
350. RM, 548.
351. RM, 501, 589.
352. RM, 1413.
353. RM, 904.
354. RM, 187.
355. RM, 983, 1137, 1375, 1386.

Conclusion

realm of heaven,[356] the company of heaven.[357] We express our confidence that the dead, who were sustained with God's merciful grace, have been found worthy to pass over into that eternal company[358] and have come safely to the paschal festivities.[359] Thus, we pray that the dying may leave the world without the stain of sin and find their eternal rest in the embrace of God's mercy.[360] We trust that God brings to fulfillment the good work he has begun in us,[361] so that we can reach the good things to come.[362] By fulfilling our duties on earth,[363] we merit to reach eternal joys[364] and to be received into the halls of heaven.[365] While on earth, we pray to merit the grace of God's redemption in heaven,[366] to experience in perpetuity the fruits of redemption,[367] to share in divine nature,[368] to know the power of Christ's resurrection,[369] to behold God for eternity,[370] to enter into the inheritance which God has promised,[371] and to be worthy to possess eternal life.[372] We hope to be numbered as fellow citizens of the saints and happy members of God's household[373] in our heavenly and eternal homeland.[374] Our final passover, our final transformation, will enable us to possess the joys of the homeland of heaven.[375]

356. RM, 488, 1392.
357. RM, 1385.
358. RM, 1316, 1410.
359. RM, 253.
360. RM, 1316, 1317.
361. RM, 1108.
362. RM, 240.
363. RM, 936.
364. RM, 391.
365. RM, 909.
366. RM, 875, 1331.
367. RM, 1047.
368. RM, 1102.
369. RM, 849.
370. RM, 858.
371. RM, 479.
372. RM, 858.
373. RM, 682, 861, 1129.
374. RM, 683, 812.
375. RM, 683.

Meditation/Journal: What have been the transforming agents, like lamb's blood, for you? Make a list of those transforming agents. What do you notice about them?

Prayer: With the blood of lambs, you transformed your chosen people, O LORD, and with the blood of your Son, you transformed the whole human race. Grant me the grace necessary to pass from what is old to what is new until my final transformation into the glory of heaven, where you live and reign forever and ever. Amen.

Bibliography

Barr, Alison. "A Meditation on Liminal Space." *Oneing: Liminal Space* 8:1 (2020) 35–9.
Binz, Stephen J. *Holy Land Pilgrimage*. Collegeville, MN: Liturgical, 2020.
Boylan, M. Eugene. *Difficulties in Mental Prayer*. Notre Dame, IN: Ave Maria, 2010.
Bruner, Raisa. "Travel Guru Rick Steves Finds Surprising Joy Staying in One Place." *Time* 196:5–6 (2020) 20–21.
Casey, Michael. *Balaam's Donkey*. Collegeville, MN: Liturgical, 2019.
Danher, James. "Truth and Liminality." *Oneing: Liminal Space* 8:1 (2020) 61–6.
"Dogmatic Constitution on the Church." In *Vatican Council II: The Conciliar and Post Conciliar Documents*, edited by Austin Flannery, 350–426. Northport, NY: Costello, 1987.
Encarta: World English Dictionary. NY: St. Martin, 1999.
Flanagan, Brian P. *Stumbling in Holiness: Sin and Sanctity in the Church*. Collegeville, MN: Liturgical, 2018.
Gitlitz, David M. and Linda Kay Davidson. *Pilgrimage and the Jews*. Westport, CT: Praeger, 2006.
Hendler-Voss, Amanda. "Restore Justice." *U.S. Catholic* 84:8 (2019) 32–7.
Hubl, Thomas. "Lean into Wisdom." http://spiritualityhealth.com.
Hudson, Russ. "Liminality and the Holy Ideas of the Enneagram." *Oneing: Liminal Space* 8:1 (2020) 67–75.
Kagge, Erling. "Five Questions with Erling Kagge." *Spirituality and Health* 22:3 (2019) 88.
Kiesling, Stephen. "The New American Love Revolution: A Conversation with Marianne Williamson." *Spirituality and Health* 21:6 (2018) 62–7.
———. "Personal Accountability in Chaos: An Interview with James Hollis." *Spirituality and Health* 23:4 (2020) 46–52.
McColman, Carl. *Answering the Contemplative Call: Five Steps on the Mystical Path*. Charlottsville, VA: Hampton Roads, 2013.
Morinis, Alan, ed. *Sacred Journeys: The Anthropology of Pilgrimage*. Westport, CT: Greenwood, 1992.
Nepo, Mark. "Our Walk in the World: Fitting Things Together." *Spirituality and Health* 22:6 (2019) 82–3.
O'Day, Gail R., and David Peterson, eds. *The Access Bible: New Revised Standard Version with the Apocryphal/Deuterocanonical Books*. New York: Oxford University Press, 1999.
Paintner, Christine Valters. *The Soul of a Pilgrim: Eight Practices for the Journey Within*. Notre Dame, IN: Sorin, 2015.

Bibliography

Poffenberger, Michael. "For Such a Time as This." Letter from the Executive Director of the Center for Action and Contemplation. June 2020.

Poust, Mary DeTurris. *Everyday Divine*. New York, NY: Alpha, 2012.

Robertson, Brandan, J. "On the Threshold of Tomorrow." *Oneing: Liminal Space* 8:1 (2020) 57–60.

Rohr, Richard. "A Big Experiment." Center for Action and Contemplation. August 16, 2019. http://cac.org.

———. "Community as Alternative Consciousness." Center for Action and Contemplation. June 1, 2020. http://cac.org.

———. "The DNA of Creation." Center for Action and Contemplation. December 6, 2020. http://cac.org.

———. "Engaged Love." Center for Action and Contemplation. September 22, 2020. http://cac.org.

———. "Fallow Time." Center for Action and Contemplation. November 12, 2019. http://cac.org.

———. "Five Consoling Messages." Center for Action and Contemplation. April 5, 2020. http://cac.org.

———. "God Uses Everything." Center for Action and Contemplation. September 14, 2020. http://cac.org.

———. "Less is More." Center for Action and Contemplation. December 13, 2020. http://cac.org.

———. "A Liminal Time." *The Mendicant* 10:2 (2020) 1, 5.

———. "My Story, Our Story, THE Story." Center for Action and Contemplation. August 28, 2020. http://cac.org.

———. "Politics: Old and New." Center for Action and Contemplation. November 20, 2019. http://cac.org.

———. "Practice: Contemplating Art." Center for Action and Contemplation. November 16, 2019. http://cac.org.

———. "An Uncreated Spark." Center for Action and Contemplation. August 15, 2019. http://cac.org.

———. "Wounded Healers." Center for Action and Contemplation. October 26, 2018. http://cad.org.

The Roman Missal: Study Edition. Collegeville, MN: Liturgical, 2011.

"*Rosarium Virginis Mariae*: On the Most Holy Rosary." In *The Liturgy Documents*: Volume 4: Supplemental Documents for Parish Worship, Devotions, Formation, and Catechesis, 525–50. Chicago: Liturgy Training, 2013.

Scobey, Annmarie. "Keep Prayer in Mind." *U.S. Catholic* 83:5 (2018) 43–4.

Senior, Donald. "This Issue." *The Bible Today* 58:4 (2020) 218–21.

Shapiro, Rami. "Roadside Assistance for the Spiritual Traveler. *Spirituality and Health* 22:5 (2019) 14–5.

———. "Roadside Assistance in the Holy Land." *Spirituality and Health* 22:1 (2019) 46–50.

Sheldrake, Philip. *The Spiritual Way: Classic Traditions and Contemporary Practice*. Collegeville, MN: Liturgical, 2019.

Walsh, Carey. *Chasing Mystery: A Catholic Biblical Theology*. Collegeville, MN: Liturgical, 2012.

Bibliography

Wright, William M. and Francis Martin. *Encountering the Living God in Scripture: Theological and Philosophical Principles for Interpretation*. Grand Rapids, MI: Baker, 2019.

Recent Books by Mark G. Boyer published by Wipf & Stock

Nature Spirituality: Praying with Wind, Water, Earth, Fire

A Spirituality of Ageing

Weekday Saints: Reflections on Their Scriptures

Human Wholeness: A Spirituality of Relationship

A Simple Systematic Mariology

Praying Your Way through Luke's Gospel and the Acts of the Apostles

An Abecedarian of Animal Spirit Guides: Spiritual Growth through Reflections on Creatures

Overcome with Paschal Joy: Chanting through Lent and Easter—Daily Reflections with Familiar Hymns

Taking Leave of Your Home: Moving in the Peace of Christ

An Abecedarian of Sacred Trees: Spiritual Growth through Reflections on Woody Plants

Divine Presence: Elements of Biblical Theophanies

Fruit of the Vine: A Biblical Spirituality of Wine

Names for Jesus: Reflections for Advent and Christmas

Talk to God and Listen to the Casual Reply: Experiencing the Spirituality of John Denver

Recent Books by Mark G. Boyer

Christ Our Passover Has Been Sacrificed: A Guide through Paschal Mystery Spirituality—Mystical Theology in The Roman Missal

Rosary Primer: The Prayers, The Mysteries, and the New Testament

From Contemplation to Action: The Spiritual Process of Divine Discernment Using Elijah and Elisha as Models

Love Addict

All Things Mary: Honoring the Mother of God—An Anthology of Marian Reflections

Shhh! The Sound of Sheer Silence: A Biblical Spirituality that Transforms

What is Born of the Spirit is Spirit: A Biblical Spirituality of Spirit

Very Short Reflections—for Advent and Christmas, Lent and Easter, Ordinary Time, and Saints—through the Liturgical Year

Living Parables: Today's Versions

My Life of Ministry, Writing, Teaching, and Traveling: The Autobiography of an Old Mines Missionary

300 *Years of the French in Old Mines: A Narrative History of the Oldest Village in Missouri*

www.ingramcontent.com/pod-product-compliance
Lightning Source LLC
Chambersburg PA
CBHW071452150426
43191CB00008B/1321